How Can You Come Out If You've Never Been In?

How Can You Come Out If You've Never Been In?

Essays On Gay Life And Relationships

By Donald Vining

The Crossing Press/Trumansburg N.Y. 14886

Books:

A Gay Diary, 1933-1946; *A Gay Diary, 1946-1954*;
A Gay Diary,. 1954-1967; *A Gay Diary, 1967-1975*;
American Diaries of World War II, Edited by
Donald Vining. The Pepys Press, 1270 Fifth Ave.
N.Y., N.Y. 10029.

Magazines:
Cruising, Sex Specialization, Meetings and Matings, and
Handling Rejection appeared in THE ADVOCATE
(sometimes under a slightly different title); *The "Mar-
ried" Gays* appeared in BLUE BOY; *Straight Talk* and
What's The Good Word appeared in GAY COMMUNITY
NEWS; *When Gays Travel* appeared in IN TOUCH; *The
Progress of Pornography* appeared in MANDATE (un-
der a different title); *Old Is Not A Four-Letter Word*
and *Where Do We Go From Here* appeared in NEW
YORK NATIVE; *How Can You Come Out If You've
Never Benn IN?* appeared in **PLAYGUY** (under a slightly different title); *Phallusies* appeared in TORSO.

Library of Congress Cataloging-in-Publication Data

Vining, Donald, 1917-
    How can you come out if you've never been in?

    1. Homosexuality, Male—United States—Addresses,
essays, lectures. I. Title.
HQ76.2.U5V56 1986   306.7'662   86-2328
ISBN 0-89594-188-0
ISBN 0-89594-187-2 (pbk.)

To
RICHMOND
This time in his rightful name

TABLE OF CONTENTS

RELATIONSHIPS:

YESTERDAY:

TODAY:

TOMORROW:

RELATIONSHIPS

Sex Specialization

Many people lament the increasing rareness of general practitioners in the medical profession, noting the proliferation of specialists who concentrate on one small area of the body or a limited range of bodily afflictions and diseases. The fragmentation of medical care is as nothing, however, to the way gays these days seem to be turning into sexual specialists. With even a quick glance at the classified ads in gay publications one sees that several concentrate their eroticism on tits, some on armpits, while some announce a preoccupation with feet and others declare foreskin to be a must. It occurs to me that perhaps the gay world could use a movement back toward holistic sex to parallel the push of some doctors for a return to holistic medicine.

In the days of my youth, well before gay liberation was dreamed of, we who were homosexual considered ourselves fortunate if in the mass of humanity around us we discovered an occasional male who shared our sexual orientation. Even then, of course, we had our druthers and certainly didn't automatically bed every homosexual who crossed our path and admitted brotherhood. We might, as I did, spurn those over a certain age or those whose physique and physiognomy did nothing to raise our sexual temperature, not to mention our cocks. If the overall lineaments and measurements coincided roughly with our notion of what was attractive, however, we generally proceeded to bed and somehow made do despite any departures from our absolute ideals of beauty or technique. Even then we sometimes found ourselves involved with people whose inclinations struck us as a bit bizarre, a bit overly focused on one approach to sex to the exclusion of all others. On occasion we might be frustrated by a trick who couldn't take our big toe out of his mouth long enough for us to put anything else in. We might even be ruined for an upcoming day at the beach by having our body marred by bruises and hickeys planted around our anatomy by someone whose lips and teeth just had to leave on us the equivalent of the World War II GI scrawl, "Kilroy was here." By and large, however, we were mostly general practitioners in those days, drawing the line at this, perhaps, and preferring that, but happy on the whole to be enjoying the favors of one who seemed to be enjoying ours.

If, during World War II, I somewhat favored sailors over handsome men in other branches of the service, I certainly never turned down an attractive soldier, airman, marine or even, in extremity, those relatively unsexy beings, my fellow civilians, if they showed interest. Some were tough and some were tender, some were hairy and some were smooth, some were tall and others slightly built, some reciprocated and some did not, a few were chatty and a few were stolid. Now and then one was decidedly over- or underendowed, but on the average they were—well, average, what else? I was grateful for them

4

all, and my notions of what can make a man attractive expanded greatly, as did my ideas of what made for fun in bed. I had long thought that my boyhood friend George and I might be the only males in the world who liked this sort of thing, and it was exciting to discover that homosexuals came in so many sizes and flavors. Strawberry might be my favorite kind of ice cream, but a switch now and then to burnt almond, rum raisin or orange sherbet was always a pleasant change.

In the decade after the war, as so many of us settled in the cities where our numbers made us a substratum of society, we may have refined our choices a wee bit, asking what someone liked before we got too involved. All we generally felt we needed to know in those days, however, was whether the person fucked or sucked, those being the two major camps into which gays then divided. Still further along in time, those two divisions more or less merged, following the example set by the corporate world. For a while we took things as we found them and came close to being unified. Nowadays, though, we seem to have splintered into preference groups and subdivisions, most of which seem to want nothing to do with the others. The breakup of the Bell Telephone System is small stuff compared with the fractionalization of the gay world. What once might have been slight preferences, more often waived than not, now seem to be prerequisites and absolute demands.

The specifics listed in the classified ads of gay periodicals dizzy me, as does the vision of how complicated cruising would have been in my day if before we took somebody home from the park or from one of the few bars then openly gay we'd had to go over a check list. By the time we conferred with the prospect as to how long his cock was, whether it was cut or uncut, whether he was hairy of body, whether he demanded verbalization or would be satisfied with a silence broken only by occasional slurping, whether he had to be top or bottom, was warm and caring or a cold fish, and could prove his age with a birth certificate, someone else would have made off with him.

Many of these questions are answered in advance these days, since nobody is as swaddled in clothes as we were then. Tank tops and shirts open to the waist make clear whether or not a chest is well developed and hairy or smooth, and if nipples are one's thing, just how prominent they are. Cutoffs reveal the legs on which we had to take our chances, since shorts were rarely worn and, when they were, were of the unflattering Bermuda-short length. Tight pants reveal the shape of the ass, as the loose clothes of the 40's and 50's did not. In addition, there are hankerchief codes, if one can remember them, and the very ambiance of many gay bars tell you a lot. Those turned on by men in pinstripe suits don't go looking for them in a leather or Levi's bar. All this is fine when one goes out cruising for a one night stand. One can nowadays avoid the occasional mismatches that cropped up in the more uncertain era of my youth. This age of specialization seems, however, to be reinforcing very particular tastes that needlessly narrow horizons. One must certainly have doubts about those who bring their sets of sexual specifics into play when placing an ad seeking a long-term one-on-one relationship. The qualifications for being the stud of one's dreams and those for being a mate for life are very different, and to a certain extent incompatible. Heterosexuals have almost never, in any era or any country, confused those factors that make for a good mate with those that make for a good mistress. Gays in great numbers now seem to be confounding the two.

Gay papers with classified ads did not exist in my youth, and if they had, I suspect I would have made the same mistake I feel too many are making today. I too had very clear notions of what I wanted, but unfortunately I could not then put them into print. If I had, and if there had been anyone out there who could have imagined he filled the bill, I suspect it would have turned out much as it does when a friend says he has somebody you absolutely must meet because you have so much in common! We would have loathed each other. It's a certainty that any ad I ran giving my preferences would not have, could not have, brought a response from the one who has been the love of my life for 40 years. He would not have seen himself as described in any way by my list of preferences, though he might have seen himself in my list of aversions. I would have said tall, to start with, and he's only 5' 9"; I would have said blond or red-headed, that being the phase I was then going through, and his hair was even then pepper and salt; I would have said politically liberal and he's conservative, canceling out every vote I've cast for decades by voting for the opposite party; I would have certainly said masculine, and he's no more butch than I am. Had I gone into the negatives, as so many ads do ("no fats, fems, beards, smokers"), I'd have certainly said, "Nobody over 32." Once this would have been 30, but as I was within a year or two of that when we met, I was starting to push my extreme limits back just the merest bit. He, as it happens, turned 41 the year we met, but because I expressed astonishment that so many of my friends were attracted to older men, he did not reveal his age for three years. I suppose I would then also have said, "Little or no body hair," since in those days I was put off by it, though I had tolerated a good deal of it in my come-what-may sex life. In fact, it was partly the hairiness of his shoulders that led me to hesitate for

7

a month after we met in a steam room before going to bed with him. Had I been inclined to be as demanding as some of today's advertisers I might also have said, "Nonsmoker, nondrinker," in an attempt to locate a totally kindred soul as pristinely free of vices as I was. This might have spared me 40 years of breathing in clouds of someone else's exhaled nicotine and tar, but I think the price would have been too great. Even if I now come down with lung cancer through no vice of my own, it will have been worth it.

Nowadays, a reader who fancies he'd like to settle down with one person might snap to attention when he reads that an Italian is wanted, as he could fill that bill, but then he might find himself eliminated from consideration by the fact that the advertiser says, in effect, that "lips that touch liquor shall never touch mine." Or he sees he must be under 30, and he turned 33 a month ago. If he decides to give up the occasional drink and lie about his age, he finds he has still more hurdles to overcome. The advertiser says he wants someone who just wants to stay home by the fire (is this character speaking metaphorically, or does he really have an apartment with a fireplace and does the chimney really draw?). This demand makes it sound as though the occasional night out with the bowling league might be resented. Besides that, he reads, he should be crazy about Judy Garland records, and somehow he's never cared one way or the other about Judy. So, the Italian who meets only one of the specifications runs his eyes farther down the column of ads. He finds an ad run by someone who lists bowling among the interests he wants shared and that looks more like it. But no, the bowler wants a blond WASP executive type, so obviously a dark Italian Catholic television cameraman won't do. Coming on an ad that seeks someone 30 to 35, preferably Latin or Italian, interested in bowling and good dinners with wine, he cries "Aha!" But the ad goes on, and he sees that he should be tall, which he isn't; should be uncut (and where on earth can one get a foreskin and have it sewn back on?); should like early morning jogging, whereas he likes to sleep as late as possible and still get to work on time; and he should also be extremely handsome, as the advertiser so immodestly describes himself (aren't they all?). A look in the mirror tells our Italian that though his mother and his aunts always said he was gorgeous, the matter might be debated by the less biased. He sighs in despair.

The specialists, at least those who claim to want a long relationship and not just a hot fuck-buddy, seem to me to suffer from several delusions. Some seem convinced that mates must share each other's interests in all particulars, having personalities that are virtually mirror images of each other; others seem equally convinced that mates must be total contrasts, a pairing of tall and short, dark and light, dominant and passive, young and old. And all this in addition to providing all the ultimate sex turnons that one might ask for when sending for a callboy. The mirror-imagists seem never to have noticed, with both gay and non-gay pairs, that many a coupled opera or symphony lover attends musical events alone or with a friend whose mate is also hostile, or at least indifferent, to music. It doesn't seem to have come to their attention that in many pairs one partner smokes or drinks and one does not, that one loves Tolkien and his Hobbits while the other sneers that that's for sophomores, that one watches endless tennis or baseball on television while the other weeds a garden that could wither and die for all his games-minded partner cares. Those who believe in total contrast on a permanent basis seem unaware of the difficulty, if not impossibility, of filling roles in perpetuity. Young "sons" grow older, and does "Daddy" then cease to love him and seek another son? "Daddy" grows older and too vulnerable to be leaned on, and does he then get the heave-ho? Those addicted originally to dependency acquire confidence and suddenly revolt against the very dependency they once wanted. Even the most dominant person has moments when he flags with the effort and wants to be able to lean on someone himself till he recovers his energies. One of the harder tasks an actor faces is sustaining a role through a long run; sustaining a rigid role in a sexual and emotional relationship is even more difficult. There is an ebb and flow in most personalities, and love must be sufficiently all-encompassing to accept variations from day to day or year to year. Those specialists whose minds are set in favor of this or that don't seem to allow for the wonderful variety that exists not only in the human race but within any one specimen of it. A relationship too inflexible to cope with this variety is probably doomed to be one of those short ones which disillusion so many gays who ask so much of others and so little of themselves.

As Charles Silverstein pointed out in *Man to Man: Gay Couples in America*, those gays who survive as couples (the nest builders) have from the outset made less of the quality and frequency of sex than have the excitement seekers; the nest builders, he found in his survey, frequently have very imperfect sex indeed, but a very rewarding intimacy and love. The shared life means more to them than the shared bed. Perhaps it is the threat of AIDS that makes so many think they can find in one and the same person the ideal roll in the hay and the ideal lover with whom to live happily ever after. If only it were that easy. Generation after generation of heterosexuals worldwide has found lust and love hard to combine in one package for any length of time. I see no reason why it should be easier for gays to attain such an elusive goal. What they need to learn is that love itself is a turnon that can make one blind even to such immutables in another person as a stature well under one's ideal requirements or a weight well over it, to skin not one's first choice in color and genitals suitable only to a human being rather than to a horse. If the specialists really want a caring relationship, as they so often say, I'd advise them to be far more open to departures from their fantasy fucks and to save all the specialization for those nights out they'll undoubtedly have eventually even if they find a mate. Fortunately, I know that whether they can make this adjustment to reality consciously or not, love has a mischievous way of making those with rigid preconceptions swallow their prejudices and eat their words. They may keep love at bay now with their excessive demands, but it's apt to sneak up on them when they're not looking, and from an unlikely quarter. Those who are impatient for that to happen will just have to open a few more of the doors they now slam shut in the faces of those who don't meet their ultimate specifications. We who grew up without the luxury of today's ability to specialize really had a very good time, believe me, as we went home with our surprise packages and found all sorts of people and sexual techniques more to our taste than we had ever imagined they would be. It was very good preparation for the many compromises that a life together requires in all arenas, from the sexual to the social. The whole gay world was our oyster, and we really didn't demand that we find a pearl every time.

Meetings and Matings

Much conversation and socializing go on during the Tuesday Volunteer Nights at National Gay Task Force headquarters. As we work on our various projects for the furtherance of gay rights, mouths are often just as busy as hands, comparing notes on a new disco, perhaps, or getting acquainted with a new volunteer. At one of these gabby sessions, I heard a regular go into a confessional vein.

"Oh, I came to New York with all the usual dreams—a great apartment, a lover with whom I'd settle down forever. Now I feel lucky to have any apartment at all, and as for a lover, well, we all know that gay relationships never last."

This is a remark I'd heard other young gays make when I wasn't in a position to cut in with a refutation, but this time I was not about to let one of our own help the straights perpetuate the myth.

"Just a minute," I said. "You're sitting next to someone whose relationship has lasted 40 years and who socializes with dozens of couples who've been together nearly that long or longer."

"Forty years!" gasped the young man who, it turned out, wasn't born until 12 years after my partner and I met. "Where did you *meet?*"

His formerly wistful eyes were aglow with new hope. That this should be his first question, or a question at all, startled me. Where and how we met had never seeemed in the least relevant to the longevity of our relationship or to that of any of my coupled friends.

"As it happens, we met in a steam room. But I don't see that as significant. None of our friends met that way, as far as I know. We know pairs together from 15 to 50 years, and those I know about met in many different places, different ways."

"Such as?" the earnest youth persisted, still on the trail of the secret that had eluded him and his acquaintances, the obscure places where those with the temperament to be lasting partners lurk.

I told him about such meetings as I then knew about, and he looked crestfallen. He had tried all such places and found them wanting. He saw now that I was not going to be able to give him the magic key to paradise.

"For all I know," I said, "some lasting couples may be forming right here at the NGTF Volunteer Night."

"Oh, sure, couples that will last all the way till Hallowe'en," sighed the sad and disillusioned one.

I smiled and shrugged at his cynicism, for though I have certainly enjoyed my long relationship, I do not view enduring liaisons as the ultimate gay experience for everyone. Some horses are created by nature to work well yoked into a team; others are born to sprint around tracks, and others to ride the range. One of the advantages most gays have is that they need not be locked into a relationship, as so many straights are, by consideration for a partner unable to earn a living or for children who need contiinuity of guardianship. It seems foolish of us to throw this advantage away in pursuit of a goal of "partnership forever," which was conceived for heterosexuals and in eras when life expectancy was half of what it is now.

Those, both outside the fold and in it, who keep mouthing the myth that long-term relationships between gays don't exist annoy me only because I know how false it is, not because I am promoting such marriages. One could easily fill an Olympic stadium with long-term gay couples. Once I have borne witness to the fallacy of the statement, however, I am not interested in advocacy. For all I know, the person I'm talking to may lack the qualifications for pairing off successfully, and I don't consider anyone doomed to unhappiness if their perhaps outmoded quest for love eternal fails.

The question of the relevance of meetings piqued my interest, however, as did the fact that I had given it no thought up till then. Now I wondered and decided to question all couples I knew or encountered to see if I found any pattern that would confirm the young man's belief that meeting places were somehow the key to romance, or my belief that they were not.

In our age bracket I found nobody else who had met their partner in a steam room. One much younger man had met his lover at the baths, but that relationship is little past the honeymoon stage, and durability remains unproven. My mate rather dislikes my mentioning the setting of our first encounter, seeming to feel that it's a slightly disreputable milieu for the beginning of such a bourgeois pair as we are now. If people's eyebrows go up when I mention it, he quickly points out that said steam room wasn't in one of the baths, which he looks down on (though I still patronize them), but in the Men's Residence Club. He also points out that we both had rooms there. True, but we had lived there for months without encountering each other in the basement pool/shower-room/steam-room complex, where indeed we had each met, and tricked with, others before. And while the name Men's Residence Club may have a respectable ring to it, the place's reputation was a good deal less lofty.

To a supervisor on the job, whom in the callousness of youth I regarded as an old auntie because he salivated over accounts of my wildly promiscuous life, I once described the place as "a combination old man's home and whorehouse." And in my diary I once noted, "There were eventually six in the pool besides myself, four of whom I've been to bed with." I mention this only to emphasize that the place was not to be confused with the Union League Club, and that since I had never for one moment fallen in love with any of my previous shower and steam room contacts, there was nothing magical about the place; the magic lay in the other person.

With a nice evenhandedness, transient rooms were dispersed about all floors of the building, and for three decades or so people checked in and out for no other reason than to cruise the washrooms, the sun roof and the pool area. As had no doubt been the case when it was a Y, the sound of a running shower heard over the transoms was sure to be quickly followed by the sound of doors opening and slippers padding towards the washroom on the way to perhaps the eighth brushing of teeth for the evening as the merchandise was surreptitiously checked out. My partnership did not start off to the romantic sound of gypsy violins but to that of hissing steam and running water; the odor was not that of a rose bower but of sweat, steam, soap and chlorine.

The fact that the Men's Residence Club was in part residential, offering inexpensive rooms to those of us just starting our careers, undoubtedly helped nurture romance once embarked upon. Having finally discovered each other, my steam room friend and I could easily continue the contact until deepening acquaintance left me totally smitten, almost literally sick at the prospect of any day that, for whatever reason, was not to contain a meeting. Propinquity and ease of access unquestionably further relationships, though the MRC did not, upon our meeting, suddenly turn into a staid little enclave of monogamy. It went right on being raffish, raunchy and full of temptations for both of us, which we did not noticeably resist. Sorry about that, young idealists!

The elegant way to meet, the one my partner would have preferred, since elegance matters to him as it does not to me, is to be introduced at a social gathering in a materialistically lush setting. A number of couples in our network can look back upon just such a first contact. Two were introduced at a brunch by friends who thought they'd be a match, and two others met on a blind date arranged by friends when both were World War II soldiers. On the other hand, my partner met my predecessor at a party with all the requisite tone but broke that off shortly after the steam room encounter in the buff, which I would call a victory of cocks over cocktails.

I would certainly have had nothing against meeting a partner at a private gathering, but not all of us have friends with the same matchmaking gifts as those who brought our friends together. So often the people we're going to like and find attractive set our teeth on edge almost instantly, partly because of a widespread misconception that similar tastes cement couples, whereas, in point of fact, it is more apt to be disparities, differences in gifts and personality, that prove complementary.

Two opera-lovers may end up fighting over whether Callas or Tebaldi, Pavarotti or Domingo is tops in their vocal category; an opera-lover encountering someone who can't abide the art form may be bowled over that the person he has just met can build shelves and cabinets with an ease that is quite beyond him. At any rate, however elegant the ambiance at the beginning of a relationship, we all know how inelegant can be the sniping, snarling and recrimination with which some of these duos come to an end.

Would you believe toilets as a cradle of romance? Certainly Barbara Cartland would never start one of her romantic novels with the two lovers sitting on hoppers in adjacent booths, edging a foot ever closer to the dividing partition and a pedal extremity next door. Nevertheless, one of the most successful couplings we know started just that way. These men, who have one of the most loving and mutually supportive relationships I know about, met playing footsie in the john of a great Midwestern university, where they were students in different departments. Many of us have played these games, responding to signals from toes wiggled significantly, passing the message on toilet paper under the dividing wall. Since the foot and a bit of ankle are just about all that is clearly visible, it cannot be considered holistic attraction that is initially at work. The shoes or sandals may tell you something (if you believe in direct correlation between size of body parts) and certain perhaps rash judgements can be made from the fact that boxer shorts, jockey shorts or no shorts are nestling in the pants down around the ankles. It isn't quite what was meant, however, when editors of romance magazines and producers of 30's and 40's movies instructed their writers to have their lovers "meet cute." In real life, though, it's a start as propitious as any other. Our friends emerged from their respective cubicles to see if they liked the rest of the respondent as much as the lower fragment they'd been dealing with. They decided they did, and within a month had moved in together. In a few more months they went through a formal marriage ceremony performed by an understanding minister.

They've a traditional wedding album to document the event. Though leafing through it might give Rev. Jerry Falwell a stroke (happy thought), to romantic gays it can only bring a glow. Despite my insistence that I don't see the point in aping straights this way, even I find myself glowing with the rest.

Toilet twosomes, I find, are fairly numerous, especially among those a generation or so behind mine. Despite the existence of gay activist groups, gay church groups and even gay dances on the university campuses of America, I find that what we used to call the tearoom brought together many lovers we know. On the collegiate scene, in fact, it definitely seems to beat out the classroom as a place of initial contact, though classes are where the longest-lasting gay couple known to us (55 years) met. Nor is all lost if one graduates without having met Mr. Right among the graffiti. We know another couple who struck sparks at the urinals of a rail terminal. Sharing condos in New York and the Caribbean, traveling abroad yearly, they now live with all the elegance that some might feel was lacking in the place and way of meeting. Sordidness lies not so much in beginnings as endings, if it ever comes to that, and I don't see endings short of death for any of the pairs who met among the plumbing.

Bars are where many seek love and lasting coupledom as well as the quick fuck, and bars, I've discovered, were where more than one long-partnered acquaintance first met his mate. Two couples well into their third decade together knew on their first night that this time it was different from previous bar pick-ups. Others a generation behind them also report having met lovers in bars, a comforting thought for those who've had too many nights when it's dogs to one side and "attitude" to the other.

The workplace, though it brings together many heterosexuals and lesbian couples, is not prominent among the places where gay male lovers meet. We do know one instance, two young men together a mere 19 years so far, who met as teenage workers in a restaurant and have stuck together through the getting of education, problems in both their families and the pursuit of prospering careers in banking. Considering the frequency of employer prejudice against gays, it is not surprising that meeting and courting in the place of employment is difficult for males. They are more apt to circle each other warily, or even put each other down, than come together as lovers, for their very livelihoods can be jeopardized if they grow too intimate. Female friendship and affection are more readily permitted, and lesbians often form their bonds on the job. Until recently they had fewer places to meet than gay males did, and therefore most of the lesbian pairs we know met in the schools, offices, libraries or whatever where they both once worked. One lover pair met side by side at a quick-lunch counter, a type of meeting I haven't yet unearthed among gay males, though there seems no reason men might not strike up an alliance over a BLT sandwich. All my mother's lesbian relationships save one (and she had many, which has always made me question the frequent lesbian assertion that they pair more enduringly than gay males) were formed in the course of her work as a book salesperson. She never moved in lesbian social circles. so I cannot imagine what other recourse she would have had in those days.

For males, the street is more promising. Two friends met at a newspaper kiosk in the neighborhood of their two apartments, cruised each other and eventually gave up separate residences for a co-op now heavily decorated with souvenirs of their joint world travels. Even foreign streets cannot be excluded from the realm of possibilities. One couple, who now own a Greenwich Village restaurant, met through eye contact on the streets of Madrid. To follow through on this sort of thing one needs at least a smattering of common language; in this particular case, the American was a Cuban emigré well equipped to deal with communication problems. Another acquaintance met his fate in a combination of street and toilet possible only in the non-American world. He and a doctor met in a Paris *pissoir* and found themselves mutually attracted; the American settled in France for good. As many a dogwalker knows, the street still offers several opportunities, and the odds on the coupling being durable are no worse, if no better, than bars, baths, parties, etc.

One thing that became clear as I inquired into beginnings is that most gay male love affairs start out as just another trick. Whether initial contact is made while sitting in a movie house and growing increasingly conscious of the warm leg that has been placed against one's own, while making purchases in a department store from an attractive sales clerk who grows flirtatious, while waiting on the curb for the crossing light to change or climbing into a parked truck, at first gay love tends to look like mere sex. It may very quickly become apparent that this time one's interest goes far beyond the crotch, that on this 200th foray a diamond has suddenly been found in the muck, but initially it is a trick much like scores that preceded it. Some times, as pure sex the encounter may even be inferior to many that have gone before. But deficiencies in equipment or technique suddenly seem unimportant. A chapter in Silverstein's *Man to Man*, "Excitement Seekers and Home Builders," makes the point that many couples of long standing have considerable sexual-adjustment problems. But lovers know, soon if not at once, that living together and sharing a life involves so much more than the genital relationship. One thing they may note, which differentiates this quickie from its forebears, is that the other person shares the nesting instinct without which it is hopeless to dream of going hand in hand into the future. As the movie *Taxi zum Klo* and the less realistic film *Making Love* both showed, it is hell's own work to make a go as a couple if one would really still prefer to be a roving stud.

Those who lack this instinct in youth, however, may develop it later, after a full crop of wild oats has been sown. A craving for domesticity and partnering hits different people at quite different ages, as another overheard conversation at NGTF made clear. Said one, "I'm only 24 years old, and I don't want to settle down with one person yet. I want to run around for a few years." Which brought the rejoinder, "Well, I'm 24 too, and after three years of being out every night, I'm tired of running around. I've had all that. I want to stay home with somebody." He really is too young to despair. All is not yet lost.

Of the couples I know, about half settled down quite early, in their teens or 20's and occasionally say wistfully, "I've really hardly been without a lover, never had any free time at all." The other half, to whom I belong, were this side or that of 30 before they met their romantic destiny. In some cases they got the running around out of their system, taking a little more time about it than the 24-year-old did. In other cases, perhaps, career demands made it impractical to continue pouring as much time and energy into one-night stands and serial pairings as these demand. Perhaps, as with straights, witnessing others settling down created cravings to follow suit and at last made "having someone to go home to" more important than "having someone to go home with." At any rate, deducting length of relationship from known or surmised age, it is clear that many of the bonds were forged after considerable freelancing, failed earlier attempts or, perhaps, late emergence as a gay. If my sad and embittered fellow NGTF volunteer can just hold on a few years, he may find the field of nesters greatly enlarged, the outlook for the domestic setup he craves quite improved. He must never suppose such pairings can't and don't exist. The more I think of it, I believe it was an understatement when I said long-term gay couples could fill an Olympic stadium. We could pack the state of Rhode Island border to border, with an overflow into Massachusetts and Connecticut.

The Married Gays

In the last five years several books have been devoted to durable gay couples. Despite them neither the straight nor the gay would seem to have any realistic idea of the large numbers involved. The straight world grows smug and the gay world despairing about the myth that gays cannot maintain long intimate relationships. Either gays are too busy pursuing the hedonistic life of bars and baths to read Silverstein's *Man to Man*, Mattison and MacWhirter's *The Male Couple*, and other such books, or they feel they represent just a few exceptional cases. In point of fact gay marriages are neither exceptional nor a new phenomenon. They have been around at least since the Victorian era.

Some gay marrieds, have actually had a religious ceremony performed by a sympathetic, renegade clergyman; most have not, and many would not even if they legally could. These latter didn't so much consciously embrace gay marriage as slide into its patterns without fully realizing what was happening. Whether they made vows at the outset and perhaps went on a honeymoon trip makes little difference. By the time two men have shared lives and living quarters for a decade or so, they think of themselves as married. They tend to move in social circles of other similarly mated gays, which is why both the straight world and single gays can be almost unaware of their existence.

A few overzealous gay propagandists like to claim that such same-sex marriages are virtually indistinguishable from heterosexual couplings, apparently feeling that this lends them respectability. Considering the present sorry state of marriage in the straight world, it would be no particular compliment to a gay marriage to say it resembled that of heterosexuals, but at any rate it is at best only very superficially the case. Gay mates may have the same devotion to each other as a straight pair, may share many of the same domestic concerns, but there is a world of difference.

Gay marriages could never be much like those of straights as long as they lack legal sanction. The fact that there can be no joint income tax returns, no automatic inheritance, and that in case of serious illness, even a remote blood relative may have a gay mate banished from the hospital room is just the beginning of the list of differences. Such marriages do not produce children, for one thing, though one partner may have at least occasional custody of children produced by a prior, more traditional marriage. The lack of reproductive capacity may remove some of the elements that makes straight marriage abrasive, but it also removes the glue that holds some straights together through stormy weather, and the freshening variation that children's growth through various stages brings to heterosexual marriage.

Above and beyond all that, however, gay marriages involve two males. Both are brought up with the expectations of achievement that are early laid on every male but on few females; neither one is brought up as women are, to be subservient to a mate. Furthermore, both partners have male libidos, which puts a whole different face on the question of sexuality. Rarely do gays pair off for reasons of financial security (men are not good at giving or taking support from another man over an extended period of time). They don't marry for prestige for it confers none (though they may be attracted to power and celebrity, they cannot, as many women do, forge an identity from it that satisfies them: they must strive for their own.) For obvious reasons they don't contract a gay marriage to continue the family line, a motive for many straights, nor to escape from a boring job into the easier and loosely defined role of "housewife." Gays become a pair not to gain a house-keeper or a breadwinner, but simply because they prefer to go through life with each other rather than with anyone else.

They stay together for the same reason rather than because their church frowns on divorce (most churches would be delighted to see them part), because they don't want to traumatize their children, or because they can't afford to pay alimony and maintain a new household at the same time. However much squabbling a gay couple may be seen and heard to indulge in, and they are far less inhibited about this than most husbands and wives, they are nevertheless together because of love and love alone, for there is no other reason for their existence as a couple.

In earlier eras some gay couples spoke simperingly of their mates as their "husbands" or their "wives" and occasionally played out what they saw as these roles. By and large the people who bandied these words about so much turned out in the end to be not so much married as "playing house."

The couples who proved most enduring seldom used such terminology or even saw themselves in such roles. One might do more cooking than the other, one might be a slightly stronger breadwinner, but they didn't assign roles or names on the basis of who did what in the straight world. Dominance certainly existed in some of the pairs when it came to decision making, or even in bed, but this was never assumed to be a gender-related trait. Gays were aware, even if the straights themselves tended to overlook it, that in the heterosexual world many a man macho in the business world was a cowering pawn when faced with the woman who dominated the home and thier social life. Though lesbians were often enamoured of the "butch-femme" role-playing, gay men tend to accept each other as androgynous beings who, however effeminate they might seem to the straight world, were inescapably male in physique and just as inescapably male in what society expected of them and in what they had been taught to expect of themselves. Years of indoctrination left them unable to accept an identity which was only a reflection of their mates, unable to be dependent and not strive, unable to live comfortably with themselves if they simply earned their way through life by dusting a bit, cooking a roast, and making their body available to their mate if they weren't plagued by a headache.

If partners in gay couples don't generally, except in a campy moment, speak of each other as their husband or their wife, neither do they refer to each other as "my lover" unless they are very young. Some long-standing couples, bowing to the custom of the day, somewhat reluctantly adopt that term now ubiquitous, but it doesn't come very naturally to their lips. When the longer-lasting gay marriages were contracted, "lover" was what the dictionary still defines it as, " a person in love, esp., a man in love with a woman." Women then had lovers, men did not. While it was certainly awkward to go on calling a mate a "room-mate" or "My Friend" for years, "lover" seemed just as awkward. Particularly in view of the fact that most gays who have been partnered for many years have had, in that time, some side affairs. These people who come into and out of their lives while their mate remained seem to gay marrieds more properly called "lover." It seems to them a word better applied to passing fancies than to permanent mates.

Most of the gay marrieds have made their own rules. The law sets up no codes for the formation or dissolution of such pairs as it does for heterosexuals. Neither, of course, do the various churches. They have created their own rituals, one of the most important of which is the celebration of anniversaries. The more the world insists that gay relationships don't last, the more of an occasion an anniversary becomes. If they don't celebrate these from the outset, they soon will after hearing even their own kind ooh and aah at the news of how long they've been together. They may think they are just doing what comes naturally in being together at first, but as their longevity as a pair is made much of by others, as it invariably is, they begin to accept the common view that maybe each additional year together represents some sort of positive achievement. The longer they go on, the more excited younger gay couples (or even singles) may get about their anniversaries, seeing the pair as role models that promise similar fates for their relationship. It is sometimes a bit of a problem for a gay couple to decide just what date to celebrate as their anniversary—the date they met, the date on which they first had sex, or the date on which they committed themselves to each other.

Gays being gays, this may conveniently all have transpired the same day, or it may be a bit more widely spaced. It only has to be decided and agreed upon when one feels the partnership as such really began. Since no legal or religious knot was ever formally tied, with a few exceptions, gays are free to celebrate whatever they choose. Nobody much cares as long as they can in some way help celebrate the flouting of the myth of gay love being only short term.

Gay marrieds, however domestically settled, are only relatively withdrawn from the sexual arena. Those who confine their sexual activity to their mates throughout a long shared life are rare. They accommodate their male sex drives in various ways by mutual agreement (or in the beginning, sometimes by fierce disagreement). Sometimes they search for other couples with whom they can have a foursome but it isn't easy to find a couple who seem equally attractive to both partners. It may be that they can at least agree on *one* person who turns them both on and have a threesome. Since many single gays are attracted by the very idea of becoming part of a couple, not to mention by the variety of positional possibilities and simultaneities for three in bed, candidates to make up a trio are not difficult to come by. Again the only problem is getting both partners to agree on who is or isn't an appealing trick. One man's meat is sometimes his partner's poison.

More prevalent are those who have their separate flings with people. They may agree on one or more separate nights out a week or a month or operate on a more informal basis, taking opportunity as it comes. If their work separates them for periods of time, these absences from each other may give them all the time they feel they need to explore other sexual possibilities. Generally neither discusses what the other may have done separately, rightly regarding it as irrevelant to their basic relationship. Sometimes they quite frankly and openly embark on a side affair which, if it does not go on too long or get too serious, the mate may tolerate. By the time a couple has weathered a few of these extramarital affairs on both sides, they may have learned that often a flood of new love for the enduring partner can come over them.

As they age, gay marrieds often wax romantic, even sentimental, about partners they have been snapping at and sniping at for years. The threat of impending loss suddenly makes them very tender with each other. At this stage they can be very misleading role models for younger coupled guys who imagine they were always this kind to each other. The older pairs can mislead their juniors by pretending to themselves that their marriage was always as serene as it now seems to be and quite possibly is. Almost certainly it wasn't. Gay couples on the point of rupture should rest assured that virtually no gay couple reaches their 30th anniversary without having had a full quota of sullen sulks, wild rages, doors slammed in anger, tears, near separations and actual splits later repaired, plus many crises in their bedrooms, from the death of desire for each other, to ill-timed entrances in the midst of orgasms not their own.

Silverstein's book *Man to Man: Gay Couples in America* says that while sex is important to many of the couples surveyed, it is not the major factor in long-term coupling. That tends to be shared interests and a desire to be coupled and those temperamentally suited to gay marriage are little inclined to throw away a good thing because their partner had a roll in the hay with someone else.

Whether today's gay couples will prove as enduring as

those who've now been together so many years is a question. So is whether they should bother to try. For one thing, gay couples of earlier eras were in many cases modeling themselves on heterosexual role models now considered inappropriate. Life is long, love sometimes short (and not just among gays, despite all propaganda to that effect). There is no real virtue in gays' staying together just for the sake of staying together. If love has really died, there is no good reason why gays should remain locked in partnership. There are, after all, no children to upset by separation, no religious vows to flout.

Judging from the classified ads in many gay publications, many gays have very unrealistic expectations as to what gay coupledom involves and they are almost certain to be disappointed in the reality. Some advertisers are plainly scared, hoping to avoid AIDS and other diseases by settling down to a lifetime of fidelity with one. While two forming a partnership now might confine their sexual activity to each other for a year or two and that might be enough to carry them through to the time when a medical breakthrough finds cause and cure, they almost certainly are not going to find a mate who is forever physically true or one who will so everlastingly satisfy their own sexual needs that they never wander from the straight and narrow path.

Others who advertise are in the grip of new romantic attitudes that lead them to believe someone exists somewhere who can fill all their needs. No such person exists for anybody. Those gays who most succeed at marriage to other gays, like those heterosexuals whose marriages endure, don't really expect too much of each other. When the film of love and passion peels off their eyes and they discover the flaws in each other and the drawbacks of being paired, they tend to shrug and get on with it rather than breaking up and looking for a better match with someone else. Realists are the ones who succeed at gay marriage for they know in their hearts that any other pairing would be no better in the end, would run the same course from initial passion to calm accommodation. But since the initial stages of passion are such a high, there is no reason why gays should feel guilty if they have serial relationships. They would simply be following other role models in the straight community, role models perhaps more valid than the old ones for this era of longer lives and greater emphasis on the sexual.

While no studies I know have demonstrated that gay marrieds have greater longevity than their footloose brothers, it's probable that they do, just as is statistically the case with married straights as compared to singles. Going through life in pairs has many practical advantages, even if not quite the ones young romantics may have in mind. It is beneficial to one's health, not only to have someone to look after you and take over some duties when you are ill, but also to look after in turn when poor health makes them falter. Even after the sexual element of the pairing has nearly or totally disappeared, the love and affection that remain can be one of the most effective medicines known to man.

Gay marrieds are fiercely protective of other gay marrieds, knowing the problems and rewards as well. In the old days they tended to mediate disputes and mend matches but with the rise of therapists they are more inclined to keep hands off and just hope that all problems are straightened out in time. Those who have endured for a matter of decades as a couple seldom had the advantage of such gay-orientated therapy when they passed through their times of crises. Love and common sense had to serve in its place and fortunately a good supply of both was on hand for thousands of partnered gays. The number who have made it to their thirtieth, fortieth and fiftieth year together would astound not only the gay world's straight detractors but the gay world's own cynics. It's time gays, at least, stopped giving lip service to the falsehood that gay relationships never last.

Gay marriage is certainly in as healthy state as straight marriage. That may not be saying a lot, but straights have no cause to be smug and gays have no cause to be unduly depressed. Given the extra hazards we face, the ease with which we can walk out of our informal bonds, gay relationships have a mighty good record of durability. Take it from one whose 40 year relationship is of not remarkable length in our large circle of gay "married."

Handling Rejection

Thanks to educational outreach by some gay organizations and militant agitation by others, gays these days tend to have to deal with fewer kinds of rejection than they used to.

In this more muscular era fewer gays may have to endure the old gym-class and playground rejection that made it a banner day when team captains chose us athletically klutzy sissies next-to-last rather than last. Various court decisions are making it harder for the military to reject men and women simply for declaring themselves homosexual, if they cannot be proved to be acting on their sexual impulses. This is at least a step up from its past policy of throwing out of service even Purple Heart winners like Leonard Matlovich. (Of course, we've known all along that enough gays have served in various branches of the military over the years to make up sufficient legions to have defended ancient Rome from the barbarian hordes.) If societal rejection is diminishing under persuasion and pressure, however, there remains just as much personal rejection in the gay world as ever.

Even the most gloriously attractive among us are not immune to this, for nobody is everybody's type. Adonis and Apollo themselves might well be chilled by "attitude" if they showed up in gay bars, baths and discos. Their classic beauty might easily gain them disdainful looks from gays who prefer their men older, younger, chubbier, hairier, darker or kinky in some way. The number of gays with truly catholic tastes in men is relatively small, and it seems unlikely that this sort of rejection will ever disappear from the scene. While we can work to end the rejection we may meet from established religion, businesses, the military and our families, we had best learn to accept as inevitable a certain amount on the personal level. Too many of us take it far too much to heart, sometimes crippling ourselves emotionally and sexually by avoiding all chance-taking out of fear that we may be rejected.

Of course, we will be rejected from time to time, just as we will reject. The sky will not fall, however, if we are, not even the piece of sky above our own little self-centered world. There are, thank God, millions of gays in the world, even if one regards Kinsey's estimate of 10% of the population as a bit high. If 14,500,000 find you not to their taste, about 500,000 will see you as delicious. That ought to be enough to keep anybody's engagement book (and bed) well filled.

Furthermore, not all rejections should be considered final. Some result more from circumstance than from sexual indifference. A pass turned down on Monday would not necessarily be turned down on Friday, when the object of your lust did not have to report to work early next morning. Surely, each of us has reluctantly passed up many people who proffered their favors at an inconvenient moment—when our energies were depleted by a hard day's work or a hard night's orgy, when we knew we had imbibed so much that we would be unable to rise to the occasion, when in a short time we were due to meet friends, family or a lover.

Many reasons for rejection do not reflect negatively on you at all. I always find it useful to remember the rueful wails of friends who bemoaned their inability to respond to a pass because they were: (1) wearing long johns against the winter cold and feared they'd look ridiculous and unsexy when they stripped before highly sophisticated urban types, (2) recovering from an adult circumcision or surgical repair of their anal tissues and feared pain would outweigh pleasure for another week or so, (3) were temporarily impotent from medication, (4) had a visiting nongay relative at home. I also remind myself of the times when I could not respond to a come-on at the moment because: (1) I had just come from a long sweaty day's work and felt in need of a bath, (2) my mind was so involved in the preliminary working out of an article or play that I felt desexed, (3) I absolutely had to finish revising a manuscript to meet a deadline and could not allow myself to heed sexual impulses, even for the likes of a young Alain Delon.

Though folk wisdom has always said, "Opportunity knocks but once," this is fortunately not true when it comes to sex. A second or third or fourth try may very well find that whatever situation interfered with success the first time no longer exists, and he who demurred before may now, with all obstruction removed, leap at the the bait.

So often we don't give the other person a chance to reject. We reject ourselves on his behalf, convincing ourselves that he would not accept us, so there is no use trying. We figure these beauties are too dazzlingly wonderful to approach, and when this feeling is rampant in bar or bath, one may see these delectable numbers go sadly home alone. It is an irony often remarked upon by Hollywood sex goddesses in interviews, that they spend many lonely nights at home because everyone figures they have more dates than they can handle. An even worse irony is that sometimes when you avoid the real object of your interest in order to escape rebuff, and turn to someone infinitely less well favored by nature, figuring he's got to be grateful for your attentions, the second choice rejects you so firmly and cruelly that it takes you a long time to recover from the blow to the ego. Condescension can lead to every bit as much rejection as does aspiration. I long ago learned to go after the one I really want, no matter how much above me I may feel he is. My record of success is such that I recommend this principle to everyone. If you head for the heights, the competition will fall away simply because so many other people are making such a bugaboo of the possibility of rejection, instead of giving it its true weight and shrugging it off. Believe me, a frog can be every bit as fussy, every bit as frosty, as the noblest prince.

Doubtless, those of us who work in the arts are one up on those who hold regular jobs, for professional rejection is a constant with us. A writer who has sent out a manuscript 15 times and got back only rejection slips with no encouraging comment, and then finally sells it, has had a valuable lesson in marketing and persistence. So has an actor, dancer or singer who has gone through countless unfruitful auditions before acceptance. Whether we start out with different, hardier temperaments or simply learn to live with rejection, certainly most of us are less phased by sexual rejection than are the general run of gays. Compared with a rebuff dealt to our ambitions and our livelihood, what is a mere sexual rebuff, where there is nothing more at stake than a night's roll in the hay?

Unless, of course, the rejection comes from a lover of long standing. I don't mean the temporary rejection that comes from a headache, weariness or a desire to concentrate on a 56th viewing of *The Wizard of Oz*, but the rejection that becomes so consistent as to add up to a permanent "no." It's an unfortunate fact that lust seldom dies with a convenient simultaneity in both halves of a gay couple. There is a period after desire dies in one partner when it persists in the other. Unlike the rebuffs encountered while cruising, which should be flicked off the ego as casually as lint off a blue suit, a lover's ultimate rejection is heavy stuff, which calls for soul-searching.

One has to ask oneself, when dealing with this sort of rejection, if the relationship has enough to offer in domestic comfort to be worth continuing without sex. Do love and affection seem to remain, even though sexual attraction has evaporated? Does the possibility of sex outside the relationship seem to exist, or is the partner going to be a dog in the manger, jealously claiming proprietary right to a body he no longer wishes to avail himself of? According to the Blumstein and Schwartz book *American Couples*, gay male couples handle the problem of sex outside the partnership better than heterosexuals or lesbians. Not only do they have outside sex sooner and more often than other types of couples, but they are less likely to split because of it. All this looks very calm and reasonable in the book's statistics, but it doesn't mean there isn't a lot of stormy weather in these relationships when it begins to happen. Neither does it mean that the rejection isn't painful for the one most in love, the one first to be rejected by his mate.

There are only two courses open for the one rejected: to hang on until the pain dies, or to split and run. Many, perhaps too many, choose the second course. They refuse to accept the advice of older, more experienced couples that this is what most of gay coupledom comes to in the end, a relationship steadily richer in affection and companionship but one in which sex plays a weaker and weaker role, if any at all. If sexual attraction has less longevity than romances would have us believe, certainly pain at rejection fades even sooner. Though for a time it may seem like the end of the world, it need not even be the end of the relationship. It is more the norm than the exception that eventually most coupled gays would rather have sex with outsiders than with their mate. Tens of thousands of gay couples have weathered the crisis of a mate's rejection, thought not necessarily without having emotional scars to show for it.

When we speak of rejection, we probably think first of that we receive. Later, if at all, we may give a thought to that which we deal out. If we give too much weight to the first, we give far too little to the latter. Everyone has a right to reject someone whose interest he cannot return, but he could do worse than remember the golden rule and do as he would be done by. From the time I entered the gay world, I envied those who were suave and kind with their rejections; I hated those, myself among them, who acted outraged that someone should aspire to sleep with such a paragon. It is as easy to be gentle as brusque, as easy to appear flattered as indignant, when declining advances. Only now and then, when dealing with crudely persistent types who are deaf and blind to all subtleties of rejection, does one have to utilize the haughty glower, the stinging words. The fact that so many gays go in for overkill in rejecting is what makes many others unduly timid, unreasonably sensitive to what we should all view as nothing but a minor setback in our sexual venturing.

If gays need to reevaluate the sexual rejection they receive and inflict on others, they need even more to search their souls about the social rejection they indulge in. An appalling rate of anti-Semitism, anti-feminism, racism and anti-lesbianism persists among gay men, even as they protest the rejection they receive as a group from heterosexual society. I've heard far too many gays who would bridle if someone said, "I hate fags," say bluntly, "I hate cunts. And dykes are the worst." Lesbians often express their low opinion of males in general and of gay males in particular. We will never be able to eliminate sexual rejection from the gay world, and there is no reason why we should. There are those bleeding hearts who seem to think a disinclination to sleep with teenagers, blacks, older people or heavier people represents anti-democratic discrimination; that we should give our bodies as an act of charity if for no other reason. This nonsensical policy would deny us our sexual preferences; it patronizingly assumes that an ample number of genuine admirers don't already exist for the young, old, dark-skinned and chubby, though of course they do.

What we can try to eliminate, each gay man starting with himself, is any inclination to discriminate socially and to bad-mouth the minorities and women, a majority in society but underprivileged. Instead of turning looks of withering scorn on those who have the boldness to aspire to our beds, we should save our disdain for those with the chutzpah to ask the world for tolerance of gays while displaying so little of it toward others.

When Gays Travel

The purpose of travel is to get out of a rut, get a new perspective, have one's preconceptions shaken up. This isn't always a comfortable experience, however, and for gays it can be upsetting in ways unknown to most travelers. Those who know exactly where to find their fellow gays in their home setting, who know just how far they can go in openly gay behavior without offending local mores, can find themselves suddenly returned to the feelings of uncertainty they once had in these matters. That old sense of being alone in one's cravings and sympathies can close in and depress, especially if traveling with a tour group. Those who have built a comfortable world in which their everyday associates understand to one degree or another that their sexual and romantic life is unorthodox may find themselves once again objects of prurient curiosity and even derision.

In America it is the general expectation that a male be married by a certain age and if he is not, he is expected to have a good explanation for his single state. If of Irish extraction he is given a certain lee-way, the old-country custom of late marriage and living at home into one's forties being well-known; all non-Irish, however, are expected to mate early, and with females, or to account for their singleness in socially acceptable ways. These do not include the fact that it is the humpy bus driver who makes you drool rather than the single females of the party who are so eager for vacation romance.

Perhaps if Reaganomics deepens the Recession into a Depression there will be a raising of the age at which American society expects marriage or cohabitation, an assumption that perhaps one is waiting to find and get established in a good job. One can't count on much tolerance on this score, however, if the tour one is taking is an expensive one. Disapproving faces will make it clear that the cost of the trip might better have been spent on Tupperware and a washing machine to start some woman off on the household of her consumerist dreams.

Organized tours, which many feel they must utilize for their more far-ranging vacations, invariably contain a preponderance of females—young office workers who fell for the brochure showing each young female surrounded at the bar or pool by at least three handsome swains, widows and divorcees devoutly hoping for a second chance—and the single male not disposed to escort, let alone flirt often finds himself on the spot. If he discovers in the group another gay male with whom he begins to share bus seats and perhaps even a room, they had both better be pretty young if they hope to avoid disgruntlement in the female contingent. Pretty young or very, very amusing. The ability to charm or amuse does, in many cases, get gays off the hook for having dashed so many hopes. A high percentage of gays has this ability to entertain but it isn't granted automatically, unfortunately, to all with our sexual proclivities.

The proliferation of specifically gay tours has been a boon to some of us, but are not for all. For those whose interests run to cathedrals as much as to cocks, a gay tour based on the lurid possibilities of Amsterdam, Hamburg, Copenhagen, Berlin, etc. may be too limited in geographic range and sightseeing content. Certainly those of us who are true travelers don't want to limit ourselves endlessly to that itinerary nor are all of us rugged enough to be drawn to rafting the rapids of the West. Conservative gays may also find that these gay tours provide more culture shock than would a temporary immersion in the world of straights. In addition, energy is apt to become depleted if one attempts to sightsee all day and drink or trick all night; one may soon find oneself enjoying neither the daytime nor the nighttime activities.

Traveling with a gay group does not, in any case, solve all problems. Sometimes they are simply a sub-group vastly out-numbered by other charter groups sharing plane, bus, ship or hotel. Our numbers are large but not large enough to give us exclusivity very often. The rest of the world (Iowa Meatpackers, Memphis Volunteer Firemen's Auxiliary, Sun City Arthritis Club) is apt to be along for the ride. Even if the ambiance is totally gay there can be discomfort. If female white-collar workers approach touring with unrealistic expectations, so do many gays. When booking they imagine the entire party will be made up of ravishing and available gays. On assembly it is discovered that a certain number are accompanied by a very vigilant partner, that some are outright dogs, that others cannot break their habit of giving attitude, hurrying to reject before they can be rejected.

Gays have always had the capacity to be as unkind to one another as any straight could ever be.

Traveling with a mixed group one may find other gays who have booked the tour either rush at one in vast relief, camping it up and exposing one's gayety sooner and less subtly than one would wish. On the other hand, one may find the other gays, as I did on a Mediterranean cruise, the most aloof members of the group, perhaps afraid you may lack discretion, perhaps fearful that you have ambitions to dally sexually with their traveling companion, perhaps simply in such an early stage of their romance that they are totally absorbed in each other. Whether the group be all gay, part gay, or totally heterosexual, it is still possible to feel oneself the odd man out.

Traveling alone, as I did for many years before my partner had an equal amount of vacation, suits the loners among us quite well. It is a challenge to plan and manage our own trips, to control our own time and divide it between sightseeing and cruising according to the richness of possibilities of each in a locale, and according to our energy supply. If the cruising be done abroad, however, there are little difficulties like the language barrier and concierges who keep a beady, suspicious eye on who goes in and out. If sex without much communication is satisfactory, the language barrier need not stand in the way of a good time—there is an Esperanto of the eyes and hands. One can also bone up on the gay vocabulary before leaving home, forgetting that useless nonsense about your aunt's pen. The linguistically lazy may rest assured that "Wow!" as one regards basket or buns will be universally understood, as will "Mmmm" when the right nerve ends are being worked over.

The concierges are a rather stickier matter. Tricks I picked up in Mexico and Paris, wily sorts, got round the gorgons by saying they were my brother, or cousin, studying abroad. To pull this off requires bravado, at least a remote family resemblance, and no past record of having been brother or cousin to too many previous temporary residents of the hotel. Furthermore, doubts are apt to set in no matter how much chutzpah is shown on passing the guardians of the hotel's chastity and there may be follow-up phone calls from downstairs, or even knocks at the door, which do nothing to improve the joy of sex. Staying in gay hotels in cities where they exist gets round this problem but here getting enough sleep can be difficult, what with the sound of all those feet padding to the shower room every time water is heard running, not to mention the moans, groans, and cracking of whips in the room next door.

Traveling with a partner has its own set of problems. Sooner or later, and probably the former, one is going to get from heterosexual fellow travelers that old smirk-accompanied question, "Which one of you does the cooking?" as Mr. and Mrs. Missionary Position try mentally to fit each of you into the picture of partnerships modeled on heterosexual norms. Whether or not it is true, none of their business in any case, the best answer is "Both of us," with a manner that puts the question down as irrelevant. If feeling bitchy on that particular day one can counter "And in your house?" though this runs the risk of bringing on a self-righteous lecture from Mr. M.P. on the God-given gender roles. One can run into this kind of nonsense even when not part of a tour party, just from the kind of Americans at adjacent cafe tables who like to open conversation with "It's good to hear somebody speaking English." Americans at home or abroad are endlessly inquisitive about private lives.

To escape this kind of thing my partner and I have discovered a great solution. Though mostly we have traveled by ourselves through Europe and elsewhere there are certain areas of the world where this is not practical—Russia, Egypt, and China, to name three—and where practicality dictates signing up as a member of a tour group. It was on a cruise taking us to the Greek Isles and Troy, however, that we discovered the clue to unembarrassed, comfortable travel for gays, whether single or coupled. Go with a British group. Unlike the sexually naive and excessively busy-body average American, the English do not pry. This was made clear to me when I, as American and inquisitive as the rest of my countrymen, made the social mistake of asking a Britton what a temporarily off-the-scene fellow traveler did for a living. One saw the question stiffen the British spine as he replied, "We wouldn't think of asking. We take people as we find them when we travel."

And so, I discovered then and subsequently, they do. Signed on another year with a tour of Egypt operated out of London, we found ourselves accepted without question, without attempts to judge our income and social status from our address or our work situation, and without the slightest curiosity as to which one of us did the cooking, with all that implies to certain minds. The British do their homework before they travel, know what they are going to see and why, and reserve their curiosity for the wonders of the world rather than for the private business of their companion travelers. Even the fact that we were immediately spotted by two British gays in the party and spent much of our time as a foursome didn't seem to raise any eyebrows or alienate us in any way from the rest of the group. Never have we made so many friends with whom we keep in continuing contact as on that trip. I recommend the British as travel companions for gays single or coupled. Their legendary tolerance for eccentricity extends to being unmarried at any age and even to the occasional public snits of male lovers.

Speaking of which, a word or two about the perils of an overdose of each other's company. This is not exclusively a gay problem as husbands and wives suffer from it too, but it can never be forgotten that with a gay pair you are dealing with two male egos and two male libidos, a very different kettle of fish from your ordinary husband and wife. The trouble can start at home, where a partnership that lasts through the years lacks the constant freshening brought to ordinary marriage by the fact that children's growth and development pretty much assures that no year is quite like the last. Unless some effort is made, one year of a gay relationship may be all too much like the last. Travel can help provide some renewing difference. Travel together, or travel separately. Perhaps one wants a month on a dude ranch whereas the other prefers a visit to Spain. If there can be no agreement that one's dream will be fulfilled this year and the other's the next, the world will not end if for the space of two to four weeks you go your separate ways. The world will not end and the relationship may not end nearly so soon.

If there is agreement on where to vacation, however, it must be borne in mind that you will be together far, far more than you are the rest of the year. Without a working day to provide you with respite from each other, the quarrels may come earlier and earlier each day until it's a question of whether you can manage to get your teeth brushed in the morning before testiness breaks out. To avoid this it might be wise to plan before departure that each day will contain some time apart. This may be to pursue sightseeing interests not shared equally, simply to be alone for a while, or if it's mutually agreeable, to pursue sexual adventure. The sight and sound of two gay lovers sniping at each other snottily is somehow a sorrier spectacle than a husband and wife on the outs, and few handle it as well as wives habitually do. No use souring an expensive vacation with sulks and slaps. If the time apart is to be used for tricking, it's well to have agreed beforehand how much of this is to be tolerated. This is an area that can be touchy since equal opportunity isn't always easy to come by. But abroad as at home, a good trick on the side can make one amazingly tender for a while with one's partner.

An occasional purchase of an unexpected small gift for the lover while on one's private time can also do a world of good in healing breaches and calming Travel Temper. If the gift doesn't melt his heart it should at least spike his guns. If he keeps on being sulky, guilt feelings may at least make him come to hate himself as much as he does you.

Though gays may not have quite as much disposable income as we are reputed to have, since more of us have children than the outside world realizes and since married siblings often insist that as the ostensibly single member of the family we should bear the burden of looking after Mommy or Daddy, we do travel earlier in life and more often than most heterosexuals. If partnerless, travel offers us the possibility of exotic romance. If coupled, it offers relief from possible stagnation. Whatever the hassles of coping with the snoopy and the stuffy, with cruising frustrations, with gay guidebooks whose information is to a certain extent bound to be out of date in a world of shifting sands, it's all eminently worth it.

Gays bring to travel a certain elan. The strangeness of not

quite belonging (which makes some Americans abroad desperate for the sight of a bottle of ketchup or blue-rinsed hair) is a sense we gays have grown up with and grown used to. We may find, indeed, that in many areas of travel interest in our sex lives go less against the social grain than they do at home. In Arab countries the sight of two men holding hands will not bring frowns; in France the sight of men kissing will not turn heads; in Greece two men without women at a taverna table would be a norm. Just as Americans went abroad during prohibition times to escape repression of alcohol, gays now often travel to escape sexual repression. They may run off to such pockets of tolerance as San Francisco, Key West, Provincetown or New York—or they may go further afield.

One of the rewards of being unencumbered by extended family is that we can start traveling when we still have reserves of youthful energy, and libido enough to enjoy the human landscape as much as the geographic and architectural one. Once we locate the gays in a vacation spot, we get a sense of universal fraternity that can be very comforting.

Go for it.

YESTERDAY

How Can You Come Out If You've Never Been In

Many gay men of my generation are amused when we hear younger gays claim that after the Stonewall uprising, closet doors all over America swung open and thousands of us suddenly emerged. Closets were where some of us stored our drag, or where others stashed the porn pictures laboriously collected in the days when they weren't available in newsstand magazines, but few of us had ever spent time in them ourselves.

When the term "coming out of the closet" was first coined in the '60s, it seemed a marvelous metaphor for acknowledging one's homosexuality. Now, however, many gay men speak of their fellows as "closeted" if they don't make repeated announcements of their sexual orientation to all the world —family, co-workers, friends, employers. If being liberated truly requires constant broadcasting of one's homosexuality, then some of us who were young before Stonewall might be found to have been closeted. We, however, didn't see it that way. In fact, many pre-Stonewall homosexuals were in many ways more blatant than gays today. We lived not in closets but in an underground world that had many parallels with the life of a drinker during the fourteen years of Prohibition.

Those who liked their liquor were not, in that era, remotely like the secret drinker who has not acknowledged to himself or to others that he is an alcoholic. They of course did not tell the local revenue officer that they were about to accept delivery of a case from their bootlegger, they didn't offer the address and the password needed for entry to their favorite speakeasy to just anyone, and they probably didn't tell the aunt who was a mainstay of the Women's Christian Temperance Union that they were going on a "Booze Cruise" out beyond the 12 mile off-shore limit to which Prohibition extended. Their party invitations didn't put in writing a promise that the hosts would make bathtub gin for the occasion, but those invited certainly knew they wouldn't be drinking root beer and Moxie. At football games and other spectator sports they would take their flasks openly from their pockets and swig what was well understood not to be Coca-Cola. Drinkers knew who among their friends and acquaintances was a "dry" and who was a "wet" and left the drys in relative ignorance about the drinking they were doing while whooping it up with the numerous others. With a similiar discretion gays of earlier decades spoke openly of their homosexuality to those they thought could handle it, letting others draw their own conclusions. By any sensible definition this is a far cry from being closeted.

It was with a good deal of insouciant flair, indeed, that most pre-Stonewall gays lived. Of course there were those who cringed, covered their tracks with insincere attentions to women, even contracted marriages of convenience. They were vastly outnumbered, however, by those who defied the societal taboos in almost exactly the same ways that drinkers had done during Prohibition. Even the speakeasy passwords had a parallel in the gay world. Through a grapevine whose tendrils extended everywhere, word went around as to which bars were meeting places for gays, which theatre balconies were gay cruising grounds, which restaurants had heavy gay and lesbian patronage, which photographers would develop the nude snapshots that ordinary photo labs refused to print. Just as the drinkers of the prohibition era enjoyed mocking and defying the forces of the law, so we relished the sub rosa aspects of gay life, feeling we were outwitting our opponents. Gay bars and baths could be raided, yes, as speakeasies and stills could be raided and even demolished by revenue officers. When they were, the scene of action simply moved elsewhere. Or perhaps, if reformers were satisfied that action had been taken, things started up in the same spot again after a week or two of quiet. The sexual drive, like the thirst for stimulants, is not one that the puritans of the world have ever been able to suppress for long.

Nor did gays skulk about in the pre-Stonewall days. They camped, hooted, hollered, and constantly flung defiance at the straight world. Many of today's gays, especially those so eager to gentrify the gay liberation movement and assimilate themselves into staight society, might well run into their closets and pull the door shut if they encountered a flock of their predecessors, who were often much gaudier and bawdier than most contemporary gays. Some of us did indeed avoid their flamboyant company, wince at their behavior, and try to merge indistinguishably with the run of humanity. Most, however, did not. We did not see ourselves as set apart from straights only by our sexual orientation.

We conceived of ourselves as far superior beings—wittier, quicker to appreciate everything cultural, more sensitive, and if nature gave us the slightest assist, more stunning to look at. As drinkers were "the fun people" of the Twenties, we gays thought of ourselves as being way in front of the pack. Our lives would have been too circumscribed had we let ourselves blend into the crowd. We might not have been noticed by our fellows. Without a press of our own, or clubs and organizations, we had to be easily detectable if we were to be taken into the network. Even those of us who were not given to campy behavior nevertheless made sure that no one mistook us for straight.

When gay men went out in public they generally made sure to wear a bit more jewelry than was then considered proper for males, and to wear a fairly noticeable cologne, which John Breadwinner stilll didn't deem masculine. This identified one as gay without in any way getting one in trouble with the law. They couldn't hang you for moving through life in a cloud of Canoe or wearing a silver identification bracelet long after the veterans of World War II had removed them. But gay people didn't make themselves conspicuous to attract only the attention of their peers; they wanted straights to notice too—to notice and envy. They wanted society to realize that this bright and beautiful being was one of those whom they derided as "queer." It might be said that gays before Stonewall, long before Stonewall, went beyond gay pride—to gay arrogance.

The gays now thought by some to have been closeted didn't whisper about their lives in public, either. They might confuse the straights by using women's names when they gossiped in restaurants ("Oh, Vivians's such a fickle bitch. She's had more husbands than Gloria Swanson") but they didn't lower their voices. On the contrary, they might very well play to the gallery. Looking out of the corner of their eyes, they might hide their meaning in gay jargon and camp innuendos but at the same time they wanted people at least to suspect that these laughing creatures were the outlaws.

"I adore seafood. Gorge myself whenever the fleet's in. But I can't abide fish," they might say, and any gay man would instantly know that the speaker was turned on by sailors and turned off by women, while the puzzled Mr. and Mrs. Readers Digest, listening in, would assume this was a discussion about food preferences. "I can't be bothered with jam," one might say and those not in the know would conclude that he liked only butter on his bread, never imagining that he was really saying he didn't suck men who felt above reciprocation. Even the presence of a policeman would not intimidate the campers. Gays were very showy in their talk earlier in the century. They simply used a language of their own and enjoyed using it in front of the breeders in much the same way that blacks enjoy confusing whites with jive. If a canny straight understood or thought he understood what they were really saying, the attitude of gays was "So sue me!" and they went on their merry way.

And a merry way it was, by and large. The same young gay men who erroneously assume that earlier generations lived out their gay lives in deep secrecy also imagine that they must have lived guiltily and unhappily. Some did, of course: some still do, gay liberation notwithstanding. The truth is, however, that many thousands of older gays are assailed at intervals by a deep nostalgia, not just for youth, but for the conditions of gay life in their youth. They loved the feeling that they were living dangerously, out-witting a thick-headed heterosexual world which imagined it could instantly detect a queer though surrounded by many it never suspected. They thoroughly enjoyed meeting a fellow gay for lunch and dishing gay gossip, surrounded by straights who understood neither their body language nor their coded words. They relished the sheer exhibitionism in which they would sometimes indulge when traveling in packs large enough to put their detractors momentarily in the minority. Their fun was often feverish, but it was fun nonetheless. Today's generally more sober gays may never know anything quite so intensely enjoyable as those defensive feelings of superiority.

"Gay" was not a word homosexuals applied to themselves much before the 40's, but gay in the old sense was a word well suited to the life we lived. We did not need drugs to intensify our sexual experiences. After childhoods in which some of us felt isolated, we were delighted to find a whole sub-culture of others like ourselves, not to mention the delight of finding that there were so many gorgeous men eager to climb into our beds. Gay friendships were as comforting as gay sex. Part of the fun of making a sexual conquest was rushing to tell our friends about it. "So you think that marines can't be had? Well, my dear, last night I proved you wrong. Now the next Everest looming before me is to make it with a cop. You have? You lie in your teeth. Well, tell me all about it and don't leave out a single detail."

Some segments of the gay world made a big thing of drag parties, others settled for "hat parties," confining their drag to women's hats of oulandish fancifulness. But most gay men contented themselves with their best masculine attire. We did not dress down for social gatherings as gay men do today. In the sexual marketplace of gay parties, we wanted to look our best. This was especially true in the late '40s and early '50s when a generation who had lived through the drab years of the Great Depression and World War II sought any occasion to don their fine feathers.

Not only was most gay life in the decades before Stonewall not lived behind closet doors; much of it was exceedingly public. Nowadays one cannot easily distinguish between gays and straights in opera or dance audiences. In the pre-Stonewall era, however, assimilation was hardly the goal of most of us. Since there were no known instances of police raids on cultural events, all stops were pulled out as far as costume and grooming. The hairdos and outlandish clothes many gays wore were not to be equaled until the punk rock era. Sequins in bleached and lacquered hair or in the eyebrows and eyelashes were one way to call attention to oneself.

There were also beaches where flagrancy was as common as dune grass. Feeling protected by their very numbers, gays might put on impromptu drag shows, drawing part of their audience from nearby "family beaches." A few gays might huff at parents misguided enough to bring children to these spectacles. Others would busy themselves making gay life look enviable, exaggerating their laughter and their affection for each other so that the curious visitors might trudge back to their picnic hampers in glum dissatisfaction with the way their spouses had neglected their bodies.

There was, perhaps, less hostility shown us in those days than now. Since no one was pressing for gay rights, conventional society felt less threatened than it does today. Straights assumed that gay romances had the same longevity as a butterfly's existence, and since they scarcely realized that more masculine gays existed, they felt superior. The same kind of mentality that is threatened by feminism is likewise threatened by gay liberation, especially now that gays flaunt bodies that make so many straights look like wimps. Police aside (and they always lag behind general cultural attitudes) there was not nearly the virulent opposition to gays in the '30s and '40s that there is now. Gays weren't asking for much, it's true, except to be allowed to go their own way in peace, and by and large they were allowed that.

Of course there were those who trembled, who lived in fear that some outrageous queen would by word or mere association unmask them. To protect themselves they might become the most virulent of witch-hunters. Many of us suspected that Senator Joseph McCarthy and his juvenile side-kick Roy Cohn were just such types. No amount of tolerant legislation will ever free some people from their personal demons. Nothing much has really changed as far as that goes. One still cannot serve in the armed services or some branches of the government if openly gay, but in all American wars many thousands of us have served and have, furthermore, had a high old time doing it. To paraphrase Dorothy Parker, if all the men who had gay experiences during World War II were laid end to end, I wouldn't be surprised. In their loneliness, servicemen needed companionship and sympathy, in the housing shortage they needed a bed for the night when on leave, in their all-male world they needed sexual release. Thousands of gay men volunteered to give them all three at once.

Nobody can deny that there have been many advances in gay life. The creation of gay periodicals openly sold on the newsstand, the existence in many cities of porn theaters and bookstores catering to gay people, the formation of peer groups on many college and university campuses are just a few. The idea that we are less closeted than in earlier eras, however, looks a bit dubious to those of us with a long perspective. More of us now look and act just like straights. I suppose that's what the majority of gays wanted all along but I suspect it may be a new way of being in the closet. The widespread opposition in the gay community to having drag queens and leather men in the gay rights marches and the tendency to read all men attracted to teenagers out of the movement, betray a craving for respectability. It makes one wonder if we earlier gays weren't a lot more open and bold. Effeminacy and the love of youth seem to be scorned by gays today even more than they were by the straights earlier in this century.

It may be commodious, walk-in closets that today's gays live in, but closets they are, nevertheless. Some of us who are up in years are credited with being "survivors," people who have coped with what are imagined to have been terrible and scarring times. The truth is, they weren't terrible times at all, and among my contemporaries I hear much more longing for them than deploring of them. Those of us who wanted to pair off did so in vast numbers and let friends, relatives, co-workers, and society as a whole make of it what they would. We didn't slink about and we certainly didn't whisper about ourselves. We laughed till we cried—at ourselves, and at the world we outwitted. Now we laugh when we hear people talk about our having lived in fear, trembling in our closets. I daresay that walking into a bar and ordering a drink will never be as much fun for some as it was to sidle up to the sliding panel of a speakeasy, give the password, and be admitted to the noise and fun going on inside. I also wonder if being gay will ever be quite as enjoyable as it was when it was defiant, conspiratorial, and a great big joke on the straight world.

The Progress of Pornography

Hearing of the recent death of Johnny Weissmuller, I was jolted into the realization that he was unwittingly the closest thing gays had to a porn star in the days of my youth. Even before the release of his first Tarzan film, advance pictures appeared in movie magazines showing Weissmuller, body bared except for minimal loincloth. Cocks hardened from coast to coast at the sight, and I was not alone in ripping out the pictures and hiding them away for future jerk-off fantasies. We had, after all, no Jack Wranglers, Al Parkers, and Casey Donovans in those days.

There were, in fact, few opportunities to view naked male bodies under any circumstances. One could see them in school gymnasium locker rooms, of course, but gays of my time were not generally the macho muscular types of today, and didn't feel at home in such surroundings. We tended to be athletically inept sissies who spent no more time in the brouhaha of locker rooms than our mandatory gym classes required.

In the Tarzan films made prior to the Weissmuller versions of the '30s, the jungle hero had worn not only large animal skins that covered his chest as well as his loins; under them had been body stockings to protect public sensibilities from the sight of real flesh. The fact that these fleshings, as they were called, tended to sag and wrinkle destroyed any illusion that one was seeing a real body; long johns would have revealed just as much. The sight of Weissmuller actually baring his torso and displaying a tantalizing hint of buttock when the loincloth flapped in action scenes was a breakthrough of such dimensions that today's young gays can't grasp it. They've always had nude centerfolds and male porn theaters, not to mention cassettes for home use.

We must remember, too, that in his days as an Olympic swimming champion of the '20s, Weissmuller himself would have been clothed in the decorous swimsuits of the day. Not only did these have tops to cover male nipples; they also had small skirts to mask the bulge of basket and buns. It was therefore astonishing to be able to admire, in stills and in the Tarzan movies themselves, a well-developed physique more fully revealed than ever before. Well-developed, but not over-developed.

The over-developed we had already seen. There did exist, in that sexually unliberated era, the magazine *Strength and Health*. It displayed something that purported to be the male body, but in such an exaggerated condition—biceps, thighs, pectorals and veins all bulging—that it seemed scarcely human. Many gay men cherished this magazine by choice, I'm sure, and others did so for lack of an alternative. For most of us, however, the bodies verged on caricature. And they were slightly unsexy. These bodies bulged everywhere except in the place that was most sexually important. The

61

bigger the thighs, the more they dwarfed what exercise could never enlarge. In addition, the figures were so shorn of body hair, so heavily oiled to show off their definition in photographs, that one suspected they would be as hard to hold or to embrace as a greased pig at a fair.

Weissmuller's body—and that of another swimmer turned movie star, Buster Crabbe—retained dimensions that, if well above average, were still recognizably human. Until the Tarzan and Flash Gordon plots got too repetitious and silly, gays in the '30s feasted on the sight of Weissmuller and Crabbe. After that we shifted to Jon Hall and his sarong movies. If his South Seas garb revealed a bit less of his body than the jungle loincloths, his face was handsomer, and his plots initially a bit more adult.

After I migrated to New York in the early '40s, I discovered that pornography of a very crude sort was circulating in the gay sub-culture. It seemed, in fact, to have been circulating for a long time, perhaps decades. From the hairstyling and backgrounds of the pictures, it appeared that the models were Ruritanian bootblacks, lured from their cloud coo-coo land by the promise of two tickets to the Paris Exposition of 1893. I imagined someone plying them with tokay to reduce their inhibitions about shedding their clothes. A bit too much tokay, indeed, seemed to have been consumed, or else the mushroom cellars where the photography seemed to have been done were very cold, for the cocks on view were so small as to resemble Vienna cocktail sausages. The quality of the photos suggested that the photographer also had perhaps hit the bottle a bit too freely. Though lips might linger suggestively near cocks, and cocks near the bullseye of the ass, bodies never made true sexual contact in any of these pictures. There was a limit to the risks pornographers were willing to run in defiance of the anti-obscenity laws. Bodies in lewd proximity were at any rate enough for that era's customers. It would be a later, more jaded clientele that demanded actual insertion of cocks, not to mention fists.

There were, of course, no open commercial sources for any of this pornography. One obtained it, if one did, by arranging with a friend to make copies in his own dark-room. Nothing of the sort was entrusted to regular photographic labs, which would even refuse to develop beach snapshots if the subjects' swimsuits were too skimpy. Neither was it entrusted to the mail for fear that postal inspection might lead to raids and arrests.

The rest of the world, we were told, took a more broad-minded view of erotica. Those traveling abroad were therefore enjoined to bring back to their gay friends whatever pictures they might obtain and safely get past the customs inspectors. GI's returning from World War II had had no worries about inspection when they brought in copies of the obscene murals from the brothels of Pompeii, stashed deep in their duffle bags and brought out later to titillate the wide-eyed at home. Tourists were approached in the parks of Paris, Rome, or Mexico City in the late '40s and early '50s by young men who gave a quick flash of a packet of pictures cupped in their palm. "Dirty pictures?" they'd hiss and quote a price without giving one a chance to inspect the merchandise. Casting their eyes about shiftily, they created the illusion of police surveillance even when none might exist. If, after exchange of money for one of the packets, one showed a disposition to inspect the merchandise on the spot, their hisses grew louder as they made off: "Careful! Police".

Safely back in the hotel room, one invariably discovered that one had been had by these hustlers (the word did not then connote the selling of the body, but of almost anything else). In France the pictures turned out to be copies of salon nudes long withdrawn from the Louvre as out-of-fashion art, the topmost also involving a classical satyr so that at a quick glance the packet might appeal to either heterosexuals or homosexuals. In Mexico the pictures were genuine pornography, photographed shortly after the death of Montezuma and with the participants stupefied with tequila instead of tokay. What was intended as a gamy present for a lover back home always had to be viewed as a joke in the end. If taken seriously, such pornography ran the risk of turning him off sex for a month instead of lighting his fires.

The arrival on newsstands of the magazine *Physique Pictorial* in the early '50s heralded the dawn of a new day. Published by the Athletic Model Guild of Los Angeles, it presented a variety of models, few notably athletic-looking but reasonably attractive and sometimes far better than that. Since no sexual action was even implied, and all models wore posing straps, it was apparently easier to lure *attractive* young men to pose if they were stone sober. Not only was there no frontal nudity, there was also no body hair. But there was still a feeling in the air that this was disgusting and obscene. In the mid-Fifties, however, *Physique Pictorial* took the next step and published, side by side, two pictures of the same model, one before he had shaved for physique photography and one after. This tentative and seemingly timid trial balloon probably took more courage than can be imagined in our era of beards, moustaches, and flaunted hairy chests. It proved to everyone's satisfaction that sales of the magazine would not plummet, copies would not be confiscated by the authorities, and the sky would not fall when it was revealed that some men have hair on their bodies and that others like it.

With the coming of the sexual revolution, which in time spawned the subdivision we know as the Gay Liberation Movement, we at last acquired porn stills and films involving attractive models in full action. But not in any giant leap. The path out of the woods of America's puritan inhibitions was notched by heterosexuals with their girly magazines (*Playboy* was certainly a pioneer). Gays followed at a considerable distance behind. It was not that they were any less courageous, but simply that in America male genitals have always been viewed as either more sacrosanct or more obscene than the female pudenda.

In our first porn film houses of the new era we still had to endure both inferior models and inferior photography. Some kind of uninhibitor (smokable or potable) still seemed necessary to persuade the models to perform; the result was still the old problem of an overindulgence that made erection, let alone sex acts, almost impossible. One could, astonishingly, find oneself falling asleep in porn movies, incredibly bored by badly filmed shots of flat, pimply asses, concave chests, slack posture, all topped by foolish grins on faces you'd never look at on the street. I recognized, after two or three disappointing visits to the porn theaters of those days, that as a first-class fantasizer I could top the available films at no cost, mentally undressing any attractive man I encountered or conjured up in the burlesque theater of my mind.

Then came the great breakthrough year 1972. Burt Reynolds posed in the very hairy buff (though rather coyly covering his genitals) for *Cosmopolitan*. In later issues other celebrities, famous athletes as well as actors, went still further and let it truly all hang out. That same year the movie *Boys in the Sand* was released, giving us at last high-quality photography, attractive models well able to perform while sober, and a full range of action, from the romantic to the kinky. After that, the deluge.

Could we possibly live in a more delicious, lip-smacking era of porn than we now enjoy? We don't have to sit through simple-minded Tarzan films, cluttered with extraneous plot, just to get a quick look at a bit of bare butt as the hero swings from tree to tree on a jungle vine. We can now sit through porn films almost equally simple-minded and have lingering close-ups of eagerly receptive ass-holes. If it proves to our taste, we can even acquire, quite openly if we're over 21, cassettes to show at home for guests, or for our own arousal. Not only does porn now offer models to please those attracted to body hair as well as those who like smooth bodies. It even, inadvertently I fear, offers models to please those of us who don't lose interest in a man when he reaches voting age. It's not so much that the erotic film makers purposely cater to gays who prefer men to boys. It's simply that Casey and Jack and Richard and Al continue to grind out new films even though, from the standpoint of boy-lovers, they're getting a bit long in the tooth, as well as elsewhere. God knows you don't have to ply any of *them* with anything to get a performance.

We've come a long way since Weissmuller and Crabbe. We have stars of our very own. They don't move through the jungle by means of vines, but they're swingers just the same.

TODAY

Phallusies

These days, I trust, few boys are sternly warned by puritanical or ignorant elders that if they "play with themselves" they will develop pimples on the face or warts on the hand. And surely, even in the boondocks, this long after the sexual revolution few are told that masturbation will lead to insanity. If those old "phallusies" about the cock have gone the way of the Model-T Ford and men's garters, however, others still persist.

As gay baths, centerfold magazines, porn theaters, and cassettes have given us a greater acquaintance with a wide range of male types, one "phallusy" has much less credence than it had years ago, if indeed anybody at all now subscribes to it. Back then gays assured one another, (and, for all I know, women may likewise have misinformed younger females), that you could gauge the size of a man's cock by, variously, the size of his thumb, his nose, or his feet, It didn't seem to me that thumbs and noses varied nearly as much in size as cocks I'd already been exposed to, but there certainly was a lot of variation in foot and shoe size. For a long time, half convinced by this gay folk mythology passed on to me by those I considered more worldly and experienced, I took a good look at feet when cruising and passed up those who wore shoes medium to small. It wasn't that I was ever a size queen but that I'd already had some bad experiences with the underequipped. They occasionally grew physically abusive to prove that their tiny tool was not an accurate measure of their manhood. I was perfectly happy with modest cocks (as long as I didn't have to search through their bush with a bloodhound to find them) but the possessors often were not; they sometimes beat up on their more generously hung tricks, making savage use of the muscles they had pumped up in compensation. How many delightful nights in bed I and other gullibles like me may have missed by passing up those with small feet, we'll never know. If personal experience hasn't exploded this old myth by now, those who have cast an eye on the likes of Kip Noll, Jon King and other slightly built porn stars must now realize that big cocks often adorn small frames and that even huge clodhoppers give no guarantee of giant genitals.

That now outmoded notion that there was a correlation between the size of various parts of a clothed man's body that were always visible and parts that were not was absurd. Not much more so, however, than another in which many still put stock, that all black men tend to be heavier hung than whites and ever ready for sexual action. What a trauma this must now and then cause for black men of average equipment and only normal sexual appetite. I've often felt much empathy for gay blacks with as much romantic sensibility as rampant libido in their natures, for, in temperament as well as measurements, they are bound to disappoint those who harbor exaggerated and false expectations.

A cock myth that seems lodged in the minds of many straight males is that there is no penis so inadequate in size and performance that gays wouldn't line up to have a go at it. They assume that gays are so desperate to get their hands or lips on cock that no matter how unattractive the body or personality it's attached to is, a moment's relaxation of the guard they maintain against queers will lead to a stampede toward their crotch.

I tend to side with feminists who claim their envy is of men's considerable advantages in society, not their sexual equipment. There are, however, plenty of men who have enough penis envy to outfit half a hundred resentful women.

An ongoing fallacy to which men who feel underendowed still fall prey is that some magic method exists which will enable them to remedy the situation. Some simply take the matter into their own hands, figuring that exercise develops almost all other parts of the body and must surely also be the answer in the crotch. Well, it's at least fun even if futile, as generations of body builders could have warned them. Suction devices have no great record of success, and creams are a scam. The only answer is resignation to the givens of nature, realization that not everybody in this world has a size hangup, and development of other assets.

The sad thing is that today, with so many pictures of nude males available, more men than ever are beginning to feel that their perfectly normal and proportionate sexual equipment is sub-standard. Magazines such as *Playgirl*, aimed at women, show men hung as the majority of men really are. Even when shown erect, as they increasingly are, the cocks in the pages of *Playgirl* could not conceivably be used to bat a ball out into left field. In some gay magazines some might very well give an assist toward a pennant and World Series. They search out men whose genitals conform in size more to fantasy than to human averages. The balls are plumper and hang lower and the cocks may fall just short of the knees. While most men can keep a clear distinction between fantasy and reality, between freaks and the average, some cannot. Far too many men are being psyched out by uncalled-for feelings of inadequacy these days.

It is almost the reverse of the situation in my youth, when I went through the sculpture section of The Philadelphia Art Museum. I looked at the diminutive cocks on the marble and plaster casts from classical times and wondered if it was always bitterly cold in the studios of the ancient sculptors or if Nature had bestowed on me unusual bounty. Had those ancients, supposedly so liberated about the human body that their athletes competed in the nude, really been built like that or did the artists fall prey to a feeling that a true scale for male genitals would be obscene? If that was realism, then I was going to have no more regrets that I had not lived in the days when soldiers were encouraged to have a male lover in the ranks. As I've said, I'm not a size queen, but there *are* limits.

In addition to creating distorted notions of normal size, gay male porn films and cassettes also use cinematic trickery to create expectations of performance mere mortals find it hard to live up to. Filming the same ejaculations simultaneously from several angles, the producers splice the shots end to end so that it seems as though men should give almost as much cream as cows do milk. Anything that doesn't resemble Old Faithful Geyser in full eruption is thereafter likely to seem a let-down. In addition, men who don't stop to think that they are watching scenes shot at separate filming sessions put back to back in the editing, may come to wonder if they, like the porn star, shouldn't be able to produce quick sequential orgasms with scarcely a second's rest in between. In the face of this illusory productivity and durability, many men have come to feel that on a scale of sexuality from 1-10 they are no better than 1½ when they are in fact 6's or higher.

If today's porn has created new fallacies of normality, it has at least helped kill some old misconceptions. Among these is one that had wide circulation in the 40's and 50's, that the uncircumcised are automatically unclean and less sexually responsive to boot. More than one of my friends went through adult circumcision because they felt their sex and love lives were being blighted by their parents' failure to have their foreskin removed in infancy. Jew or gentile, most American males for some decades were cut and if they hadn't been, felt they should have been. Now that foreskin, like facial and body hair, has come back into fashion and with some is a definite turn-on, surely nobody needs to go through what my friends did decades ago. There were the difficulties of scheduling an operation that would not really seem imperative to employers, the embarrassment of explaining it in those modest days, and of course the pain and expense, neither of which was inconsiderable. Once it was over, all those who sought to improve their sexual lot with circumcision felt they had, so strong was the prejudice then against foreskin. Like the body hair gays once took pains to conceal or to shave off, what was once considered a liability is now flaunted. Seeing a porn star slide his ample foreskin over the head of his sexual partner's cock, seeing a variety of other foreplay with this natural appendage, has educated many people to the plusses of a part of the body they once widely believed to be a liability and a blight on their pursuit of happiness.

It's notable that foreskin appears more and more often in centerfold nudes and in porn. Those who avoid it now do so as a matter of taste, not because they believe every foreskin conceals a mass of smegma or precludes the same degree of arousal a cut cock is capable of.

Another fallacy nearly, but not yet totally, historical, is the notion that there is something basically more lewd about bared male genitals than there is about the female pudenda. Long after artists and photographers revealed the female body totally and frontally, the male crotch and its constituent parts continued to be turned away or masked with the equivalent of a fig leaf. Even if the cock was completely inert rather than in a state of erection, it seemed to be a taboo long after the female crotch became acceptable to postal authorities and other self-appointed censors. Rear nudity was acceptable years before the frontal ceased to be a no-no. The poor straights who were so zealously guarding public morals lacked the imagination to realize that buns could be as erotic as baskets and to some people, more so. Now, fortunately for those of us with catholic sexual tastes, the beauty of the total male figure and all its parts is accepted, at least by the more enlightened. We don't even reduce the scale as the Greek and Roman artists presumably did (if I underestimate their realism, poor Alexander the Great, poor Hephaestion!).

A few more fallacies persist—the nonsense that one must use it or lose it, for instance. This ignores totally the fact that men on the frontier, men at war, men bound into a marriage or relationship that has become sexless with time, seldom if ever prove to have lost their know-how or their ability to function sexually when opportunity again presents itself. There's nothing wrong with keeping the tools in readiness by whatever possible means, but certainly no one need feel desperation and final loss if for a time in one's life one lacks the time, the privacy, or for any reason the impulse. One doesn't forget how to ride a bicycle, a horse, or another human body just because one hasn't mounted one for a few years.

That age in itself will in time make one impotent is another widely held belief. The thought that we must gorge ourselves at the sexual banquet before time snatches away the feast is a pernicious one, leading perhaps to some of the excesses that undermine the health of too many gays today. Medication that sometimes are prescribed for the aged may lessen libido, as may loss of a desire for a longtime partner, but age itself is no barrier to pleasure between the thighs. Even those of us who strike the young as quite possible passengers when Washington crossed the Delaware can still manage nicely, given a crack at what turns us on. It may or may not take us a little longer, we may or may not need a longer recuperative period before we give an encore, but the age at which sex becomes impossible is well beyond most people's life expectancy. When I'm ninety-three, just throw in my path the era's equivalent of James King or Paul Newman and watch me rise to the occasion. If you've never seen coping before, you'll certainly see it then.

The reigning fallacy at the moment is that our cocks may be our greatest enemy, driving us toward danger with their willful urges. I am certainly not inclined to play down the horrors of AIDS nor the risks we run of other diseases if we model our behavior on that seen in porn, thrusting cocks just removed from anuses directly into a mouth or succession of mouths. On the other hand, in our present panic, we should not come to believe that the greatest threat to our health and longevity necessarily nestles between our legs. It may equally reside, its smoke coiling seductively upward, in our nicotine stained hand. Or in that icy glass we lift far too often to our lips, that car we drive when our coordination leaves much to be desired. As virulent as AIDS seems to be, its fatality is far from matching those attributed to smoking, alcohol, and drunken driving. Let's not turn against our sexual urges and revert to the days when we were told that to touch yourself "there" with pleasure in mind was to court acne, warts, madness and damnation. Our cocks are more often our friends than our enemies and after all, we are supposed to stand up for our friends. Just think how often your cock has stood up for you.

Cruising

Like so many other apects of gay life, cruising is quite different today from what it was in my youth. Much of the uncertainty and much of the danger that we had to accept as
part of cruising back in the '40s have now disappeared, thanks
to the sexual revolution and gay liberation, and good riddance.
Human nature being less mutable than laws and mores,
however, certain constants that create crises when cruising are
still with us and probably always will be.

The baths we patronized in the '40s and '50s (which included
the shower rooms and pools of YMCAs) were basically run for
the benefit of heterosexuals, and one had to seek out the gays
among the nude bodies by noting who lingered in the show-
ers a lot longer than need be. If they soaped and rinsed, soaped
and rinsed, with special emphasis on the crotch area, one could
be reasonably sure that here was someone who was ready to
have their private parts go public. The soap customarily used
in shower rooms was Ivory, advertized as "99 and 44/100 per
cent pure"; fortunately, the purity of the customers was a lot

lower. Nowadays gays have their own bathhouses, and though personal sexual preferences will always make 100% availability an impossible dream, rejection will not be accompanied by an outrage that brings down on one's head the management at least, the police at worst.

Similar changes have occurred in theater cruising. Those theaters which the gay underground of the '40s whispered to be "wild," a code word to indicate highly fertile cruising ground, were never exclusively or even chiefly patronized by gays. Most people were actually there to see Irene Dunne or Loretta Young in whatever. Even though a man left his seat rather often to go to the men's room, there was no certainty that he didn't simply have bladder problems, and even if it became clear, side by side at the urinals, that you both were on the sexual prowl, the door might at any time swing wide to admit a straight customer who scowled at those who lingered too long. Worse yet, one was never sure that a new wave of reform might not be cresting and that the movie patron so busy trying to turn his short subject into a full-length feature wasn't a plainclothes man out to entrap. Nowadays, in the gay movie houses that have proliferated, one knows that Jack Wrangler and Al Parker aren't attracting nongays the way Errol Flynn and Tyrone Power once did, and that anyone there to see a movie entitled *Great Balls on Fire* or *Clean-uncut American Boy* shares one's sexual orientation without question. Now and then, cops may enter these theaters to deal with a captured pickpocket, but they no longer seem to get periodic feelings of discontent with the level of payoff. Today's gays, mercifully without knowledge of yesterday's dangers, not only don't get the pains of fear and tension in their back that I still get at the sight of a cop in a gay theater, they don't even miss a stroke. They have never seen handcuffed gays dragged roughly down theater balcony stairs, pale with terror at the threat to reputation, career and their previously unbruised body. May none of us ever know that again.

Bars too are very different. For the last five decades and probably longer, in metropolitan areas there have always been bars known for a clientele that was heavily, if not exclusively, gay. For much of that time, however, these bars were few in number and lacked the specialization rampant today. Young and old, preppy and macho (we didn't have the words but we had the types), S/M and drag queens, all had to share the same few bars. As they tended to dress alike, one had a much greater problem then than now sorting out those who had sexual tastes similar to, or complementary to, one's own. Between Western outfits, leather gear, handkerchief and key codes, there should be fewer mismatings than we used to suffer in my time. Besides, we speak right out these days and don't hesitate to ask, "What do you like?" if the speciality of the house or costume clues haven't made this clear.

Ah, yes, it's all much easier these days, and yet for all the changes that have made the gay world almost unrecognizable to those of us who came out just before, during or shortly after World War II, there are those problems in cruising that are apt always to be with us.

There is, for instance, the problem of being too tall, too burly, too generally intimidating physically to make it with the timid or cautious. One of the beauties with whom I briefly and unhappily lived before Mr. Right came along used to come home from nights out alone wailing, "They're afraid to pick me up. I wish I was a sailor again. Nobody was afraid of me then." Well over six feet tall, he may have had an exaggerated idea of how butch he looked or may not have been taking into account the fact that it took a certain amount of time for gays to adjust to the idea of men in civilian clothes being sex objects, after years of specializing in uniforms. But the problem of the oversized and heavily bicepped does exist. If they attract some for those very qualities, they frighten off others who might be the very quarry they seek. Certainly I, after one or two bad episodes, made it a principle never to pick up anyone I hadn't a better than even chance of besting in a struggle for my possessions or my life. Being six feet tall myself, even though menacing only in a jealous rage, I have now and then known what it is to feel an interested party slipping through my fingers purely because of a caution on his part, possibly growing out of past bad experience.

Failing to make a connection is a minor matter, however, compared to the difficulties that can crop up after all seems set.

It hardly seems necessary to mention the perils of overdoing drink when cruising. Surely we all know by now that the more the liquor consumption rises, the less likely that anything else will.

A word of caution may be in order, however, about less often experienced and less talked-about difficulties. An excess of talk can have almost the same effect as an excess of drink. Nongays hold to the mythology that most gay sex is impersonal, anonymous; and I suppose that gays do go for that sexual style at least as much as the millions of heterosexual men who over the centuries have availed themselves of streetwalkers, brothels and available girls from the typing pool. We insiders know that it isn't always as anonymous as all that, that even with casual tricks there can be a lot of talk, an exchange of background information about the age at which we came out, whether or not our siblings are also gay, what gay gathering places we frequent besides the one in which the contact was made, and much else. We can be a gabby crew, very much interested in our tricks as individuals even if we don't plan to see them again. Carried too far or badly timed, this can mess up a roll in the hay just as much as alcohol. It took me quite a while to learn to curb my writer's curiosity about people and to go to bed with the trick first, probe into his life and personality later. To do it the other way around can raise the focus of attention so far above the crotch that one is afflicted with an irreversible limpness, thoroughly fucking up the fucking.

One must also consider the hazards of the telephone. Some of us are confident that if we ignore the ringing of the phone when happily entangled in someone else's body, the caller will try again later and nothing will be lost. This, however, doesn't seem to be a widespread attitude among Americans. If you've gone home with someone afflicted with telephonitis, you may find yourself involved with a coitus interuptus such as sexologists never dreamed of. It's bad enough when the call is merely from someone seeking new subscribers to a magazine or cable TV, but if its a gossipy friend or a Jewish mother who wants a rundown on what her boy has eaten in the last 24 hours, you may end up with flu from lying naked and overheated, or at least lose your impulse. Either of which may happen to someone *you've* taken home if it's you who can't resist the siren call of Ma Bell.

Animals are another problem that will doubtless always be with us. When the trick you have latched onto is a real stunner, just what you have been looking for all these recently frustrating nights, you may proceed hastily to his place or yours without checking out the animal situation. That darling cat you so cherish may bring out in him a nasty ailurophobia that makes him suddenly far less appealing to you or, even worse, may set him to sneezing and wiping his eyes until he can't attend to the business of the evening. He may even begin to puff up until he looks like one of those inflatable Dutch Widows sold in Amsterdam sex shops. It may also be that the darling little dog Whiskey, though he may not postpone developments by an inconvenient need to be walked at once, before it's too late, may not take kindly to what you're doing to his master or what he's doing to you. There may be barking and occasional growls and nips all through the coupling.

Allergy and antagonism are not the only hazards animals can present, however. More rarely, there is a dog that is all too happy to have you mount his master as long as he in turn, excited by the sight, can likewise mount you. For those without a taste for bestiality this can be disconcerting, to say the least, and it's awfully hard to explain to a poodle that there's nothing personal in the rejection but that your tastes have just always run more to collies.

On the other hand, getting on *too* well with the pets of someone you've been picked up by can also be bad. Owners and pets are said to come to resemble each other in time, but sometimes the master hasn't yet achieved the level of charm of the pet. I happen to be a cat lover, and on at least one occasion I found myself doing more flirting and fondling with the adorable white cat of the household than with the still only semi-adorable owner who had brought me home. Suddenly aware that my host was pouting and harumphing about the amount of attention I was lavishing on the wrong pussy, I followed him to the bedroom to make amends. The big white cat, however, had its sense of fun and play operating at full speed by then and was of no mind to wind down. It proceeded to scamper about, making great leaps in the mock alarm that is a feline speciality, and scurried over our naked bodies until I was too overcome with laughter to be able to proceed, and my host was too angry at both of us to want to. He was one of those who take sex very seriously, which most of the time I find difficult to do.

Perhaps the commonest problems in cruising are those known only to the millions of us who wear glasses regularly. Glasses are not practical at the baths, and though perhaps less of a sexual turnoff than many who wear them suppose, glasses still have the reputation of diminishing one's opportunities significantly. Lots of us, therefore, try to increase the odds on scoring by dispensing with them while cruising. Quite aside from the peril of failing to see a step or a slippery spot, which can render one *hors de combat* for a matter of hours or weeks, there is the danger of involving oneself with someone who looked OK in the mists of unfocused vision, but who, on closer inspection, raises one's gorge rather than one's cock. You may find that you have picked up a pimply young thing, all eagerness and no skill, far below your desired age range; on the other hand, it may turn out that the number who seemed to blurred eyesight to be right in his prime is far more shopworn and over the hill than you have a taste for, or that he has imperfections that to others may be positive attractions, but not to you. There is then the problem, unless you have a callous disregard for the feelings of others, of either sleeping with someone not really to your taste or of disentangling yourself from the mess your nearsightedness has gotten you into. A visible recoil upon putting on your glasses does not come under the heading of graceful withdrawal. A look at watch or clock and the exclamation "Oh, my God, I didn't realize it was so late!" isn't too convincing but sometimes saves the other person's face and your day or evening to boot.

Though contact lenses are often a blessing and have greatly cut down on the mistakes we used to make in our semi-blind cruising, they are not without hazards of their own. They have a disconcerting way of coming out at inconvenient moments, and your trick's idea of sexy fun probably doesn't include crawling around on the floor helping you look for a contact only to find that it fell in the Crisco can. Nor is it likely to improve anyone's evening if you go searching for it through the hair on your trick's chest, like a squinting monkey delousing its mate.

Those who are mated have special cruising problems all their own. Not all lovers go for threesomes, and if they do, it can still be difficult to reconcile two different tastes. While lovers argue over whether a blond is truly toothsome or too young and green to be of interest, the prey could be snatched by another predator, making the question moot. Or, both partners might agree that they've spotted something that would grace and enliven their bed only to find that their quarry has no taste for group activity or is attracted to one but wants no part of the other.

Cruising in a partner's absence is something else. If it's been a while since you've been out on the town solo, you may suddenly realize that you've forgotten techniques of effective cruising or even that there are any. You may also discover that the walking dream whose gaze hooked onto yours is a romantic looking for that ideal mate, not a one-night stand, and that he is pretty disillusioned to learn you are indulging in what he views as "cheating" on a partner. Furthermore, he is unlikely to be pacified when you explain that nothing and nobody could really come between you and your lover, since this reassurance only serves to diminish his sense of his own powers of attraction. Though one doesn't customarily mention the existence of a partner unless dealing with the highly sophisticated, evidence of his existence is likely to abound in shared quarters and will raise questions even if at some point years of habit don't lead to accidental references to "us."

As to lovers' absences, they aren't always as long as anticipated. Neither do all cute tricks have their orgasms as fast as you hoped or take their departures as soon as they've had them. Unexpected confrontations may or may not upset the returning lover, may or may not bother the interloper, may or may not fill you with guilt and embarrassment, but these side excursions always have the potential of turning into situations that are sticky in more than the literal sense.

With all the problems that might, and sooner or later almost invariably do, arise, it hardly seems worthwhile cruising, does it. It does? I was sure you would say that. And I agree. What church bingo is to Catholic ladies, cruising is to gays: a gamble that pays off only now and then, but which is fun in itself. Nothing worthwhile in life is without its difficulties and risks. Why should Cruising be an exception?

Straight Talk

In these days when the Moral Majority and other adversaries are on a rampaging campaign to drive gays back into the closet, at the very least, most of us realize that it's crucial for the gay world to unite. What fewer seem to realize is that it is equally necessary for gays and lesbians to mix freely in the straight world, to be conspicuously contributory to society and to have our virtues properly credited to us rather than entered mistakenly in the ledger of the public mind in the column of the straights. Not only can we not afford to shun any segment of the gay community—the nellie queens, the S & M leather types, the boy lovers, the lesbians or whatever turns us off— but we can even less afford to hold ourselves apart from the straight world or to move about it in disguise and wearing masks.

Just as the women fighting for women's suffrage had, in the end, to depend on men to grant them access to the polls since there was no way they could vote their own rights into being, so gays and lesbians are ultimately dependent on the straight world to bestow on them their civil rights. Even with the diverse segments of the gay and lesbian world working together in a Utopian unity, the whole lot of us would still be a minority. A sizable minority but definitely a minority. There is no possible way we can win our rights except by persuading the straight world that we deserve them. Such persuasion is highly unlikely if we merely exhort from barricades; we must mingle with heterosexuals as openly gay co-workers, neighbors, and friends until vast numbers have their eyes opened as to how little the great majority of us conform to negative stereotypes.

Straight people who do not know, or do not know that they know, any gays, can accept all the mythology about us that is paramount in the propoganda of our enemies. If, however, they have been dinner guests of a gay or lesbian couple, have worked beside us in full knowledge that the mate or lover we were meeting after work was of our own sex, have entertained us at parties where we proved no less charming, intelligent, and considerate than the heterosexuals , they simply cannot thereafter be persuaded to go along with the Jerry Falwells and Anita Bryants of this world. They are not going to believe that their children or the republic are going to be corrupted by people such as the gay male or lesbian neighbors who were so concerned and helpful during their recent emergency. Neither are we gays going to believe all straights are our opponents when we number so many as friends and acquaintances.

Prejudice of all kinds—against blacks, Jews, Catholics, women, or gays—can exist only if one's contacts with the minority in question are limited. The moment one knows large numbers of people in any ethnic or minority group, one sees how various they are, how few fit the myths. It becomes almost impossible to finish perjorative statements such as "The Irish always—", "The Italians always—", "Old people always—"

because so many exceptions come quickly to mind that one's tongue is tied. The sooner gays who mix with straights but hide their gayness end their masquerade, the sooner those out but ghettoizing themselves rejoin the world at large, the sooner will the straight world be won over to the justness of our cause.

By and large people take one at one's own evaluation. If one radiates self-confidence and self-respect, the vast majority of people will conclude that the confidence and respect are warranted. Trying to hide one's gayness leads others to suppose there is something that needs hiding, something we are right to feel guilty about. If, on the other hand, one behaves as though one's sexual orientation is nothing that should concern anyone but the parties involved, both the educated and uneducated classes tend to conclude that it's a matter of no moment to them. Just as the crowd tends to accept one's own view of one's attractiveness, intelligence, success, or failure, so it will smell a sense of guilt and pounce upon it or it will detect a sense of casual self-acceptance and go along with it.

I speak of accepting one's "sexual orientation" rather than "sexual and affectional" orientation as we are nowadays encouraged to say because I devoutly hope that nobody in the gay world really confines their capacity for affection to the gender toward which they are sexually drawn, nor to the age group with which they might be sexually involved. Affection is something I hope we can all radiate for grandparents, aunts, uncles, cousins, teachers, neighbors, co-workers and others with whom one would not for a moment consider sexual involvement. Invariably the more affection one feels and displays, the more one receives; consequently, affection freely felt and expressed for heterosexuals will pay huge dividends in the crunch.

One cannot, of course, live one's whole life simply to advance the cause of gay rights. If straights were the ogres gays sometimes see them as, it would be too much of a sacrifice to fraternize with them. Since their numbers include such a lot of terribly nice people, however, it is no hardship to mix in their world and draw them into ours. It is, instead, a pleasure that enriches our lives as, we hope, we enrich theirs. And we have so much in common. I know all the arguments about "gay" meaning an entire lifestyle and not just sexual orientation but there simply is not a "gay" way and a "straight" way to enjoy music or to play tennis or tend a garden, have an operation, grieve over a dead pet, or go on a diet. The lifestyles have their differences but they are not all-pervasive and are far fewer than their similarities. Gays and straights alike have problems keeping their bank balance straight, choosing investments, coping with elderly parents, protecting their property from thieves, dealing with appliances that don't function properly, and so much more. If we think of ourselves too much and too often as beings apart from the mainstream, heterosexuals cannot be blamed if they begin to accept this assessment. It behooves gays and lesbians to remind themselves of the many areas of common concern they have with the straight world so that the straights may also be reminded.

There is a lot of ralk about "homophobia" and I certainly would not deny that it exists but I have almost never seen the term "heterophobia" though I feel there is almost as much of that about in the gay world. I think the latter is just as unwarranted as the former and that a first step to the abolition of "homophobia" is the abolition of "heterophobia". What, after all, is there to be afraid of? In what way is the fact that a person is straight a threat to the essence of our being? We can't, even in our most promiscuous and indefatigable years, sleep with everybody and 99/100ths of our personal relations are nonsexual so in most interpersonal transactions sexual orientation is completely irrelevant. If we want people to be unconcerned about the nature of our sex lives we must start by being unconcerned about theirs. If there is a segment of the straight world actively working to deprive us of liberties, we have at least as many enemies, and I sometimes think more, within our own gay world. Whatever kind of gay one is is sure to be viewed with hostility by some other type of gay. The knives we pluck from our backs are put there by individuals, not groups, and are as apt to bear gay fingerprints as straight.

As the son of a lesbian mother who throughout my childhood suffered professional and personal setbacks because of lesbian scandals, I am aware of the dangers of openly gay life in certain settings. I am also aware, however, of how much of my mothers' difficulty was brought on by her own hostility and public scorn of men and women who liked men. I believed as a child and believe now that if she had not made it plain that she saw them as the enemy, they would not have been the enemy. Having no inclination to view the heterosexuals of the world from her jaundiced viewpoint, and profiting by her bad example, I have never isolated myself from the straight world nor, in an openly gay life of over 40 years, felt that it needed to be feared or mingled with only in disguise. I have always felt, from my teens on, that by behaving as though homosexuality was nothing to hide or be ashamed of and was at any rate only a part of, not the core of, my life, I was helping to implant this outlook in the minds of the scores of straights with whom I was involved. I didn't proceed through life with defiant banners hoisted but the true flag was always flying and nobody seemed inclined to slash at it with the sabre of their tongue. There was even, now and then, a charming protectiveness evident among straight friends who felt I was perhaps a bit rash in living so constantly exposed. Long before Kinsey,

90

long before Stonewall, men and women ranging from burly college roommates through co-workers who were parents many times over have granted acceptance of my sexual bent. I see in myself nothing special that would confine such tolerance to me alone. I think it is there waiting for those who begin by respecting themselves and go on to respecting straights. It can never be granted to those who hold themselves aloof, who feel a man of heterosexual instincts can offer them nothing as a friend and that women with heterosexual desires base all their living and thinking on that alone.

Separatist gays do us all a disservice. They abet the Jerry Falwells of the world by doing nothing to counteract the poisonous propaganda that gays and lesbians are some sort of monster. Demonstrations, petitions, boycotts of distorted media depictions of gays, even perhaps riots on occasion, can achieve some of the freedoms to live and love as we like. Mingling with the straight world, not as a closeted gay whose virtues accrue to the credit of the straights but as a matter-of-fact, unselfconscious, undefiant gay male or lesbian, can achieve at least as much. Perhaps more.

There will always be occasions when one wants to be only with gays but a whole life need not be lived in their company. For the sake of one's own development and the good of the gay movement, furthermore, it should not. In the end the straights are the ones who have in their power to grant or withhold our civil liberties. We must face that fact and set out to seduce them (in a nonsexual sense) instead of ranting at them. More are prepared to like and respect us once they know us than some gays believe. Liberty and equality will surely follow fraternity.

TOMORROW

Old Is Not A Four-Letter Word

When I was in my mid-20's a palm-reader at a party looked at my lifeline and predicted that around the age of 50 I would be quite ill, a nervous shock possibly. "Just being 50 will give me a nervous shock," I told her.

This is a common attitude among gays, some of whom remain 29 for years, balking at public entry into their 30's like a steeplechase horse refusing to go over a fence. The notion many advanced that a waning of desire might parallel the waning of opportunity gave me no comfort in youth; I did not look forward to a life without lust. For all those who live in similiar dread that the good things of gay life end with their 20's, one now past 60 has reassuring words. They do not.

Older gays receive rebuffs on occasion, but so do younger gays. Who except those who cruise timorously has not at some time or other met with the lowered eyelids of indifference or an outright icicled putdown? The most beautiful young thing is sooner ar later dismissed as too effete, too dangerously tall and husky to risk going home with, too something or other, or not enough something else. One look at the classified ads in any gay publication makes it clear that age is only one of many things discriminated against by some gays. "No facial hair," "No fats, fems, or phonies," "Uncut only," "Gr passive, Fr active only," "Must be hard-hat or blue-collar type," "Into B/D and scat" read the ads. We were fussy in the pre-Stonewall days of my youth, but too happy to encounter our own kind in the then-uncharted gay world to be quite so compartmented in our desires. In any era, at any age, the rebuff is a familiar experience, however. I have not noted their frequency mounting with increasing age.

Even though we were a little less precise in our demands 35 years ago, ageism did exist and nowhere more flagrantly than in me. My diary is full of such remarks as, "He was all of 40 or more. I cannot get excited about older men," and "Ernest revealed that he, like George and so many others, was crazy about older men, who revolt me. Ernest's favorite is 48, God help us." I did learn from Ernest and George and others that however I might feel about it many people found age a positive attraction toward which they repeatedly gravitated. I decided then that I would stop worrying about my own age; but though I was intellectually convinced, I still had misgivings in my heart based on my own tendency to recoil. Only when by supreme irony I, the most ageist person in my circle (indeed perhaps the only one), fell in love with a man an unthinkable twelve years older than I, did I truly come to realize that turning the leaves of the calendar was no cause for trauma.

I had previously lost one or two beauties to older men

but interpreted this as a victory of power and influence. Then suddenly, naked in a steamroom, I encountered this man shorn of any sign of wealth and power, reduced to his essentials, and I found myself, against my will, reciprocating his interest. Not only was he of an age heretofore beyond the pale for me, but he had a hairy chest already graying, which, for one addicted up to then to smooth-bodied young blonds, took some getting used to. Wisely he gave me the time to make the necessary revisions and accommodations in my preconceived notions. Unlike those who had reinforced my prejudices against older men by groping and grabbing as though they had no time to waste on winning me over, he courted me gently. Confident that he would not snarl and turn on me if I failed to repay a theater or dinner date by immediately hopping into bed with him, I was able to go here and there with him, getting to know how much about him besides his body was of interest to me. Finding that his whole nature was the reverse of the irresponsibles I had unhappily lived with, I decided after a month that not only could I tolerate going to bed with him, but I very much wanted to. After 40 years we are still together and not just from habit.

Seeing how quickly I came to love him and how many still younger men I had to beat off and outmaneuver in order to hold him, I lost any remaining crumbs of fear of age. I had recurring lessons in the realities as opposed to the myths of being an older gay and learned that if one keeps in reasonable shape and operates from strength rather than weakness, the later years compare very favorably with those of youth.

This presupposes, I fear, a capacity to mature that some gays lack. It's an unfortunate fact that shallow queens some times grow old without acquiring depths to compensate for the fading of the beauty they may or may not once have had. The few older gays I encounter who are as unhappy as we are all supposed to be have mostly themselves to blame. They throw away the advantages of age and maturity in a vain attempt to remain one of the boys. They persist in trying to operate in old ways in settings inappropriate for men of their age. Taking no lessons from the straight world (not so different from the gay as some suppose), they ignore the fact that though older men may go with younger women, 60 is more apt to pair with 38 or 48 than with 18 and 60 seldom tries to make its contacts at bars for swinging singles or on beaches where they would be at a disadvantage among the well-toned muscles. Among straights December may sometimes mate with May but more often settles for September and seldom tries it with February. Some of those who complain bitterly about ageism in the gay world practice it avidly themselves, dismissing all those in their middle years as beneath their lustful notice. Certainly, I know many instances of men well up in years doing quite well in gathering chicken about them, but only those who play up rather than play down their age have much consistent success at this. By offering the nurturing concern and the financial help of a surrogate parent, they may fill a legitimate role in a young man's life. It's a rare youth who feels any need for a giggling, leering, gone-to-seed playmate who at 60 imagines that he stopped time 40 or so years ago. Neither do they need an old man consumed with bitterness and envy of youth at the same time he hopes to seduce it. The thin lips of disapproval are, like the tight lips of a miser, very unseductive.

Just as many straight men desire to bed women but have neither liking nor respect for them at heart, so some older gays hanker to sleep with youth while holding them and their lifestyle in considerable contempt. While it is unwise, rather undignified, and mostly self-defeating to ape the wardrobe, vocabulary and fashions of those a generation or more younger, it is all of those things and more to be constantly critical of them. There is no use cinching in one's waist, touching up one's hair, and concealing the chronology of one's life in an attempt to be young if one is going to blow the whole act by crabbing about jeans worn in once-formal settings, about beards and mustaches, about deafening rock music, about marijuana, and by nattering on about how much better things used to be. Neither is an older gay going to get very far by being excessively puritanical about money as a factor in love and sex.

Gays can be very uptight about not being loved for themselves alone, and those who are most uptight often have very little self that is lovable. Though I was never myself susceptible to material considerations (my beloved was neither affluent nor influential) and I am not personally generous, I can still recognize that money and comfortable surroundings and a leg up in one's career are, from time immemorial, universally accepted and valid ingredients in straight pairing—so why not in gay? Did Onassis believe for a moment that it was his looks which attracted Jackie K.? The ironbound marriage contract she insisted on must have disabused him of that notion if he ever had it. Was Averell Harriman put off by the fact that he was being pursued by a younger woman with a blatant record of having progressed from one rich and famous man to another more rich and/or more famous? No, he married her, as so many men do, with a full comprehension of how much of his appeal was stashed in a bank. Neither in the straight world nor the gay is materialism the only component in twilight matings, but a mature realism demands a recognition that it is a frequent factor the world around and not one that gays should feel superior to. It is certainly part of the strength of being an older gay that generally we are in a better position to introduce this factor into our pairing than we were when young.

Mostly, however, the older gays of my generation don't need the foregoing scolding about making their own troubles. I really encounter very little angst. Among the long-coupled, those who lose a partner seem almost invariably to find a new one after a year or two. Those who have lived their life unattached seem to locate young proteges in an unending stream. By nurturing and listening to the dreams of the young, by having the necessary mixture of aggressiveness and patience to court, by showing generosity, by opening their eyes to the attractions of men in their 30's, 40's and 50's, most older gays I know keep themselves off the shelf very effectively. Mine always having been an open relationship, I am still working the field with a high ratio of success and am amused that I lose the prize as often to a less hesitant man older even than I am as I do to someone younger. This gives me hope for the decade ahead, as does the fact that my older partner continues to attract, to turn heads and to turn his own for a second look at a beauty.

Quite aside from love and sex, gay old age has many other pleasures. So much is safely behind one. This feeling of "Look, we've come through" is one perhaps too much indulged in by some who, having survived themselves, give little financial or other support to gay activism and gay enterprise. As long as one tempers one's smugness with a little realization that today's freedoms were fought for, not handed out gladly by the straight world, and as long as one gives at least some help to those who are manning (or personning) the barricades against the attacks of the reactionaries, a certain amount of complacency can be comfortable. Threats to one's ability to earn one's livelihood are pretty much a thing of the past for those who have retired, the law grows more permissive and the world more understanding, and with a network of friends built up over the years, that sense of isolation one may have had in youth is gone. One knows, if in touch with the gay liberation movement at all, that hordes of young activists are out there fighting the battle for gay rights, losing here and there, winning somewhere else. There is access to gay literature, to gay art and to lush pornography as never before, and one can move freely in a gay ambiance without the feelings of furtiveness that were long a part of many gay lives.

The gay world has been maligned, I think, as even more ageist than America as a whole. One would think, to hear some of the mythology, that older gays were like lepers in the gay community. In every way, from the sexual to the social, this strikes me as nonsense. Socially, there seems to be considerable outreach by young gays to their elders. Publication of my diaries has underscored for me how many young gays are interested in gay history and are avidly recording, on tape or otherwise, the experiences of those who notched the trees on the paths they now follow. Getting letters from and meeting some of the young gays with an interest in gay history has been for me a very pleasant experience. So has working with much younger volunteers and staff in the offices of the National Gay Task Force and with SAGE (Senior Action in a Gay Environment), a burgeoning organization set up by young gay social workers, gerontologists and other members of the gay community for the express purpose of reaching out to and helping their elderly own.

Any older gay who has hung back from participation in gay activism because he felt his presence would be unwelcome is as wrong as those who think that since they survived there is really nothing that needs doing to secure gay civil rights. While one is unlikely to become bosom buddies with young gays, there being limits to intergenerational friendships of all kinds, one can be assured of respect if granting respect, of a sort of affection if granting affection, and of support for one's freedoms to be gay at any age, which is what the fight for gay liberation is all about. Much of the isolation some older gays feel is totally self-imposed and would end the moment they offered their time, energy and skills (not to mention money) to some of the many gay organizations they can find listed in the *Gay Yellow Pages*. These range from Cuban refugee committees to churches and synagogues and denominational religious groups on to political action groups.

Being gray and gay is quite O.K. as long as you grow up as well as grow old.

WHERE DO WE GO
FROM HERE?

Gays fifty years ago would never have imagined that one day several major American cities would have lesbian and gay community centers at which meetings were held by dozens of thriving gay organizations ranging from Gay Fathers to S and M devotees, from chubbies and their chasers to gay golden-agers. They would be startled to hear that even one city had capitulated and granted spousal benefits to gay mates, incredulous if told that a politician who had publicly confessed to an affair with a teenager of the same sex had nevertheless been re-elected. Their astonishment would be no less to learn that in Boston, of all places, as well as in other municipalities, non-gay politicians had added a lesbian or gay male to their staff to act as liaison to the gay community. If you told them that in one city gays and lesbians actually make up a majority of the city council under a lesbian mayor, they'd have found the idea as fantastic as anything in H.G. Wells then-new book *The Shape of Things to Come.*

Gay theater-lovers from earlier decades, seeing literate and non-explicit plays about lesbian triangles closed by censorious New York officials, would scarcely believe the list of theatre offerings on and off Broadway today. Used to plays with titles like *Boy Meets Girl* and *John Loves Mary*, they'd be startled to find a musical comedy and no less than three dramas prospering which aren't, but could be, titled *John Loves John*.

As the gay underground of those days passed along miserable examples of pornography which seemed always to have been photographed at a drunken orgy by a photographer no soberer than his impotent-looking subjects, they'd have scoffed if you told them that one day ther would be as many as a dozen gay magazines to be found on the news-stands of major cities and freely circulating through the mails. Still less would they have believed that the majority of these magazines featured superbly photographed full-frontal nudes, not of drifters desperate for cash or zonked zombies, but of men greatly favored by nature and proud to display their beauty. The existence of gay bookstores with a sufficient gay literature to fill many shelves would have been only a shade more surprising to mid-century gays than the fact that many general bookstores set aside sections for books dealing with gay subject matter.

Naturally they couldn't imagine that gays and lesbians would be openly discussing aspects of gay life on major television shows such as Phil Donahue's. Television itself was something they had to imagine since it didn't exist for the public until after World War II. Even the use of the word "gay" to describe themselves lay in the future. In my Springtime we were still having to refer to ourselves as " fairies," "queers," "queens" or, rarely in those much less outspoken days, as "cocksuckers". If we tried to give ourselves a bit of dignity we had to label ourselves with the cumbersome word "homosexuals". That wonderful all purpose word "gay" wasn't seized upon as apt generally until the '50s. *The New York Times* still resists using the word unless it is in a quote or the name of an organization, but, then, the New York Times probably still feels daring when it uses the word "stockings" instead of "hosiery" or calls a leg a leg instead of a limb, as my grandmother always did. Even the staid *New York Times*, however, would provide gays of an earlier era with an eye-opener with their very recent occasional willingness to list a male partner as survivor of a dead gay written up on their obituary pages.

It's been an astonishing half century of progress for a segment of society which in my youth didn't realize it *was* a segment of society, viewing itself as little more than a loose association of singular, if wonderful, misfits.

If gays of the present could foresee what lies ahead in the next five decades or even the next two, would it be cause for enthusiasm and envy of young gays to come or reason for head-shaking and horror? "You ain't seen nothin' yet", the theme of New York's 1985 Gay Pride March and Rally, was ominously ambiguous. A motto that would do as well for the enemies of gays, it hints at repressions topping those of the past. The grammar even sounds a bit more like that of a redneck homophobe than of a militant gay. The double edge of this theme may, however, have alerted excessively smug gays to the possibility that backlash and loss are as possible as advance. One can never assume that anything in the world will move steadily forward. Women were comfortably unconstricted of body long before the torture of corsets. Ancient Egypt had methods of construction and embalming that were lost by subsequent civilizations. Rome at its zenith had plumbing later centuries lost the knack of. Even those too young to see civilization slide backward, at least as often as it advances, must be aware that gays recently lost to the forces of reaction in Houston rights they had thought won.

Let's take the optimistic view, however, that the gay community, insofar as it actually is a community, has been jolted by its recent setbacks. Let's assume that it will soon achieve a unity that has so far eluded it, a unity that will give it the greater clout needed to advance further. The joint fund-raising effort launched in 1985 by Lambda Legal Defense, the National Gay Task Force, the Gay Men's Health Crisis, Senior Action in a Gay Environment, and the Lesbian and Gay Community Services Center with their Gay Pride mega-raffle is a most promising step. So is the talk of mergers of gay organizations with roughly the same agenda.

Life expectancy being what it is, I won't live to see nearly as much of the world's gay future as I've seen of its past, but my imagination toys with marvelous possibilities, from the political to the personal.

Could what has happened in West Holllywood, California, for instance, take place on a larger scale? If councilmen in New York's outer boroughs continue to be obstructive to the passage of a gay rights bill, could Manhattan secede from New York as West Hollywood did from Los Angeles? Could it then elect a council with a majority either gay or sympathetic to gays and perhaps end up with a lesbian or (openly) gay mayor? Dare we envision even larger triumphs: frankly lesbian legislators, gay governors, even, perhaps, a gay president of the United States? Can't you just see the infighting in Washington as a gay president's backers jostle for appointment as Secretary of the Navy or Majority Whip? Doesn't the prospect make one drool with anticipation of the first TV interviews with the First Gentleman? The President's mate (one hopes he has one, for his own and the nation's sake, and doesn't have to require the Secret Service to supply a new kind of secret servicing) may be watched more carefully than the president himself is. The public and the media that panders to it often prefer to focus on trivia rather than matters of substance. So they may very well be less concerned about the gay president's foreign policy and economic platform than they are about the plans of the new male equivalent of a First Lady. Do his redecorating schemes pose a threat that the White House will become the Lavender House? Has the President said anything to him about the rumoured appointment of Jerry Falwell as Ambassador to Eniwetok Atoll? Is it just a Republican canard that the cause the First Gentleman will choose to associate himself with is Head Start? Does the President eat quiche or is he a man that likes meat?

With or without a gay at the head of government, perhaps we can also look forward to a day when gay men and women serve in the military with no hassle about their sexual orientation from the occupants of the Pentagon. Though it seems inconceivable at the moment , just as so many aspects of current gay life did a couple of decades ago, one can certainly hope that eventually the top brass will see that an open and self-respecting gay poses less of a threat to military efficiency than gouging contractors and generals who busily prepare to refight the last war or the war before that. It may have to start with segregated units composed only of gays and lesbians, much like the battalions of blacks who won glory in two World Wars and the nisei who proved their loyalty in World War II. Though some members of the gay community would protest against this on principle, others would rush to enlist under such conditions. Especially those who swoon over the novels of Mary Renault and wish they'd been born in ancient Greece, when soldiers supposedly were encouraged to have lovers in the ranks to whom they could prove their bravery and whom they could succor (I said succor) if they fell wounded. Gays would soon prove to the military that they could fight like demons as well as perhaps make the barracks look a little less stark with some nice curtains. Once the lesbian units were unleashed and given weapons more lethal than a typewriter, don't you just know they'd make those fighting queens, Hatshepsut of Egypt, Boadicea of Britain, and Isabella of Spain, look like wimps? Once the gay men revolted at being eternally assigned to kitchen police, can't you see them bringing the enemy to their knees? (Now, now, we're talking war here!).

AIDS will almost certainly be conquered, perhaps in a decade or less. Once it hits a few prominent heterosexuals the medical profession and the government agencies that fund research will buckle down. Once the diseases first called GRIDS (Gay Related Immune Deficiency Syndrome) are renamed the Simon-Schafly Syndrome or something comparable, research funds will outdo the government subsidies to tobacco growers. Surely it will become as rare as tuberculosis, scurvy, and polio. With the threat of AIDS and other diseases that have (unjustifiably, for all we really know) given sex a bad name gone, will long 1-on-1 gay relationships fall from favor again? Will gays readopt the emotional and romantic instability of heterosexuals like Lana Turner , Zsa Zsa Gabor, Alan Jay Lerner and Mickey Rooney? Does it matter? Wouldn't gays grace the covers of supermarket penny dreadfuls just as much as any of those straights who announce every month that they are "deeply in love" with somebody new?

In cultural life, one wonders if gays will not become so clearly dominant that the talk around the country on the morning after the Academy Awards or the Tonys will not be the award recipient who thanked his male lover, but the winner who thanked his wife? Instead of supplying a woman for a gay to escort to the ceremonies as a cover, will straights be provided with a young man for the evening, leaving their wife at home, so as not to look like an oddball when stepping out of their limousines?

It must be supposed that the computer age will have its impact on gays. Let's overlook the fact that it could make it easier to have them listed and ready for roundup in concentration camps if things take a nasty turn. Let's think of what it might do to their mating habits. Already heterosexuals are viewing videotapes made by members of the opposite sex in search of a mate; is it likely gays will not in time adopt this same technique? True, it is more difficult to shave off years from one's age, pounds from one's weight, not to mention exaggerating one's attractiveness and the size of one's equipment, on a tape, compared to a printed classsified ad. On videotape cassettes it may become apparent that if you were the apple of your mother's eye, you're possibly just another fruit to mate-seekers. Nonetheless it seems likely that the classified ad is likely to be superseded. Gays won't just be renting cassettes of old Bette Davis films and Al Parker porn, they'll be going home with half a dozen reels of personal ads on tape, personals live and in color on which the candidate puts his best foot forward, or best whatever.

Perhaps possibilities for the future of gay life also lie in the personal robot. Those who know they *should* volunteer for one or more of the gay organizations fighting for their rights, but who are too lazy or too preoccupied, could send their little robot off to stuff the mailings, answer the hotline, or picket the stereotype reinforcers. If averse to the bar scene, gays could use their robots as surrogate cruisers. A winning little creature like R2D2 in *Star Wars* could be sent out on the prowl, could check out vital statistics, sexual preferences, and favored fantasies with somebody else's robot. When a red light flashed to indicate a perfect match, it could rush home with the news after an exchange of phone numbers. With the time saved in fruitless cruising, gays could change the face of the world. If by any chance the little robot (perhaps called RU12) gets out of hand like the computer Hal in the film *2001* and tries to make off with his master's boyfriend, said master could rip out his silicon chips. Some of us in my day would have liked to disembowel perfidious friends in comparable fashion but there were laws to deter us as there probably will not be if you give a rebellious robot his just deserts.

Even if such projections of the future are a trifle exaggerated, let's hope they are at least in the direction things will truly go, that "You Ain't Seen Nothing Yet" does prove a more appropriate motto for gays than for the Moral Majority which would like to push us back to our darkest days and beyond. Elie Wiesel, pleading with President Reagan not to seem to honor Hitler's vicious SS troops by laying a wreath at Bitburg Cemetery, where some of them lay buried, showed a historical perspective lacking in too many. Listing those who died in concentration camps under the Nazi regime, he scrupulously included the often overlooked gays right along with the gypsies, jews, and political opponents of the fascists who fell into none of the other categories. In a braver, better world gays would have been demonstrating against Reagan's visit right along with the Jews at Bergen-Belsen. In a wiser, less frivolous world gays would be indulging in less infighting in their major organizations, all of which should be more strongly supported with gay dollars and manpower (okay, personpower), and would be more united. This much, at least, is in the power of gays to *make* happen in the coming years.

We've come an amazing distance in the fifty-odd years of

my gay awareness and I hope we travel at least an equal distance, at an accelerated speed, in what remains of this century. At the risk of making therapists suffer as much unemployment as steelworkers now do, let's hope that gays may universally come to accept themselves as individuals without cause for shame. May the straight public also come to view us as the varied and generally unthreatening people we are. In addition to all that, may the gay community itself come to accept those in their ranks that some of them find embarrassing, even a threat. That is, may lesbians come to accept the more forthright gay male sexuality, may gay males who pride themselves on indistinguishability from suburban hubbies stop frowning on transvestites and drag queens (who after all fought the fight we celebrate in June, with little or no help from the gentry) and may all of us together stop treating the Man/Boy Love people like the pariahs all of us have historically been. Is that too Utopian a vision? Hell, let's dream big while we're at it. I, for one, am particularly hung up on the notion of a gay president and hope I'm around for the campaign.

In Texas gays were recently criticized for presenting male strippers at a political fund-raiser but when the gay (or lesbian) runs for president that sort of thing may replace the $100-a-plate rubber chicken dinner. Can't you see the beauties like the Chippendales circulating among the guests in nothing but collars, cuffs, and their g-strings while guests eagerly compete to thrust large checks and bills into the jockstraps? It would be just like that film about the male stripper that represents almost the total acting career of President Reagan's daughter Patti. Ah, yes, the campaign chest would have nipples and maybe hair on it and what if the opposition complains self-righteously about campaign funds raised through CROTCHPAC? At least gays will finally be putting their money where their mouth is. High time.

OTHER TITLES IN THE CROSSING PRESS GAY SERIES